THE MOST IMPORTANT LESSON

THE MOST IMPORTANT LESSON

Are You Ready to Change Your Life?

GARY S. EDWARDS

THE MOST IMPORTANT LESSON
Copyright © 2023 by Gary S. Edwards

Scriptures taken from the Holy Bible, New International Version®,
NIV®. Copyright © 1973, 1978, 1984, 2011 by Biblica, Inc.™ Used
by permission of Zondervan. All rights reserved worldwide. www.
zondervan.com The "NIV" and "New International Version" are
trademarks registered in the United States Patent and Trademark
Office by Biblica, Inc.™

Printed in Canada

ISBN: 978-1-4866-2478-2
eBook ISBN: 978-1-4866-2479-9

Word Alive Press
119 De Baets Street Winnipeg, MB R2J 3R9
www.wordalivepress.ca

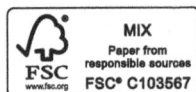

WORD ALIVE
—PRESS—

MIX
Paper from
responsible sources
FSC
www.fsc.org
FSC® C103567

Cataloguing in Publication information can be obtained from Library
and Archives Canada.

DEDICATION

First I dedicate this book to my wife, Joanne, for her never-ending love, support, and encouragement—and for calling 911.

Also, a big thank you to everyone who played an important role in helping me write this book. I have appreciated your valuable feedback and your prayers throughout my journey.

Most of all, I offer my eternal gratitude to my Lord and Savior, Jesus Christ, who through His love and mercy provided me a second chance at life in order to learn and apply *The Most Important Lesson*.

CONTENTS

INTRODUCTION

Any fool can know. The point is to understand.[1]
— Albert Einstein

Life is full of lessons.

From the day we were born to the day we die, we are continually learning. Since everything is new to us as babies, we must learn in order to grow, develop, and survive. We learned to communicate even though we could not yet speak. We learned who the special people were in our lives. We learned that there were some things we liked and others that we didn't.

Sometimes we learn our lessons the easy way and other times we learn them the hard way. Some lessons come to us quickly and others take longer before we finally understand. Some lessons we learn and forget. Some remain at the forefront of our minds. Some lessons we would love to forget.

There are some lessons we wish we had learned earlier. How many times have you said to yourself, "I wish I'd known that sooner" or "I wish I'd known then what I know now"? If you're like me, it's easy to be hard on yourself for not learning important lessons earlier in life.

---

[1] Albert Einstein, "Any fool can know..." *Goodreads.com*. Date of access: September 5, 2023 (https://www.goodreads.com/quotes/72361-any-fool-can-know-the-point-is-to-understand).

That's the point of this book.

It wasn't until I was almost fifty-seven years old that I learned *The Most Important Lesson*. I have deep regret for taking so long, but I'm relieved to have finally learned it.

My goal now is to fully implement this lesson into the rest of my life and share it with others. Nothing would make me happier than to see other people's lives positively changed by applying this most important lesson.

Would my life look differently now had I learned this lesson when I was young? Definitely! So if I can save you years of wasted time, I will have accomplished my goal.

This book is also full of smaller lessons. Please don't ignore these. They are important as well and will help to shape you as you strive to implement the big lesson.

I am not a theologian. I'm just a guy who wants to share with you the most important thing I've ever learned in hopes that it will help to better your life as it has mine.

May God bless you on your journey!

ONE

DEATH IS NOT THE END

*Every man must do two things alone; he must do
his own believing and his own dying.*[2]
—Martin Luther

February 3, 2019 was the day I died.

The night before had been a bitterly cold evening in Calgary, Alberta. Temperatures were well below -20ºC (-4ºF), accompanied by strong winds that made the "feels like" temperature reach an easy -30ºC (-22ºF).

I had planned a very special evening with my wife, Joanne. Our birthdays bookend Valentine's Day, so each year we go for a night out on the town to celebrate all three occasions.

This evening's events started with a delicious dinner at an Italian restaurant, followed by a concert. Following dinner, I stood in line to pay for my parking ticket at the outdoor lot across from the theatre. As I shivered to keep warm while waiting for my turn to pay, I thought the line would never end. I tried to ignore the bitter cold as best I could, for this Legends of Motown concert was going to be the end of a great evening.

---

[2] Martin Luther, "Every man must do…" *BrainyQuote*. Date of access: September 54, 2023 (https://www.brainyquote.com/quotes/martin_luther_385320).

As expected, we thoroughly enjoyed the concert. The talent was first-class and the impersonators sang some of the greatest songs of the Motown era by some of the best artists. People were singing and dancing in the aisles. Concerts don't get much better than this!

Arriving home later that night, we prepared to go to sleep as usual. It was midnight when we finally crawled into bed.

Strangely, I felt some mild discomfort in my upper chest, right below the neck. I thought I'd simply eaten too much at the restaurant, again, but I was sure the pain was the result of a gas bubble and would subside by morning. I just needed to fall asleep and the discomfort would disappear on its own, as it had many times before.

For the next two hours, I couldn't get comfortable. I tossed and turned, carefully, so as not to awaken Joanne, who was fast asleep next to me. I couldn't find a position that alleviated the growing pressure in my chest.

The "gas bubble" grew more and more painful, to the point that I decided it would be necessary to make a more strategic change in body position. So at 2:00 a.m., I sat up on the side of bed, thinking that being vertical would cause the bubble to rise and dissipate more quickly.

My movement caused Joanne to wake up.

"What's wrong?" she asked.

"I've got some pain in my chest."

That's all I needed to say to get the alarm bells ringing at full volume! Joanne was on her feet in no time, quizzing me about all aspects of the pain I was experiencing. She immediately googled "heart attack symptoms" and quickly moved through the list to learn how I felt.

"It's just gas, I think."

At least, that was my amateur medical diagnosis. I truly believed I was just experiencing the consequences of stuffing down a few too many garlic breadsticks. I was confident that it wasn't a heart attack because everything I had heard about heart attacks involved having feelings of heartburn, indigestion, and pain down the left arm. I had none of those symptoms.

No, this couldn't be a heart attack! My pain was more like the feeling you sometimes get in your upper chest right before you burp.

Except it wouldn't go away.

After a minute or two of sitting on the edge of the bed, the pain seemed to increase rather than decrease as I had expected. I stood up, thinking that moving around a bit might dislodge the gas bubble and we could finally go back to sleep.

I made it as far as the bathroom.

Nausea hit me like a tidal wave! I was able to raise the toilet seat just as the dry heaves started to hit, accompanied by uncontrollable loud shrieks. It was like nothing I had ever experienced! I was then reintroduced to my chicken parmesan. And yes, multiple breadsticks.

By this time, Joanne had dialed 911 and was on the phone with the emergency operator. The paramedics were on their way. The operator stayed on the phone with Joanne and continued going through the checklist of symptoms for heart attacks.

"Does he have cold sweats?"

"Gary, do you have cold sweats?" Joanne asked, standing just outside the bathroom door.

Just then, the sweats hit me as if taking their cue from Joanne. Between the violent heaves and profuse sweating, I decided this was no longer fun. The pain was also increasing in my chest—a lot!

My daughter Rochelle had now showed up after being awoken.

Joanne quickly explained to her that I was possibly experiencing a heart attack and my condition was getting worse by the minute. Joanne asked her to unlock the front door and let in the paramedics, who were soon to arrive.

When the first break in my vomiting occurred, I thought it might be a good idea to go into the living room so the paramedics wouldn't have to carry me up the stairs if things got worse. Due to our frequent trips to Mexico for work, Joanne and I had been occupying a basement bedroom while we were back in Canada. Our daughter had taken over our master bedroom on the main floor.

Upon entering the living room, the pain in my chest became unbearable. I've always considered myself to have a high pain tolerance. I had played all kinds of contact sports when I was younger and often played through pain in order to stay in games. I'd broken multiple bones, including my nose. Eight times, to be exact.

This chest pain ranked up there with the worst pain I had ever experienced. Still convinced that no heart attack could hurt this much, I assumed it had to be something else.

The paramedics arrived almost as soon as I reached the living room.

The first paramedic I encountered asked if I wanted to be examined in the ambulance, or in the living room on the couch. Still in my pajamas, I chose the couch since it was closest. I didn't want to feel the blast from the bitter cold outside.

I sat on the couch as the paramedic placed a small bag beside me. In what seemed like slow motion, I watched as she reached into her bag and started to pull out the ECG machine to monitor my heart activity.

That's all I remember.

Joanne informed me later that I was still conscious as they hooked me up to the machine and realized I was going into cardiac arrest. The paramedics had told her to get my boots and put them on me in preparation to be transported to the hospital.

At that point, Joanne said that my face went very pale, my skin turned clammy, and I began to throw up one more time. She turned my head to the side so I wouldn't aspirate on my vomit.

Then my eyes rolled back into my head and I was gone.

The paramedics quickly threw me onto the floor and began to perform CPR, interspersed with four shocks from the automated external defibrillator.

By this time, the firefighters had arrived and one of them dismantled our glass coffee table and moved it to provide the paramedics space to work.

As Joanne paced and prayed for God to be merciful and save me, the firefighters suggested she sit down in another room. She declined. She watched as they administered CPR, but then ducked into another room to continue calling people to pray. She didn't see me being shocked.

Unfortunately, no one noticed Rochelle on her knees at the end of the hallway, watching everything that was happening to me.

Eventually Joanne got in touch with a good friend of ours and said, "Gary's just had a heart attack and he's gone. Please pray!"

No sooner had she gotten that sentence out of her mouth than she heard one of the paramedics announce, "We have a pulse!"

I have faint memories, as I faded in and out of consciousness, of voices telling me that I'd had a heart attack and was being transported to the hospital.

Joanne and Rochelle followed the ambulance to the hospital. Upon arriving, within twenty minutes I was undergoing surgery to have two stents placed in my main "widowmaker" artery. Tests showed that I had a seventy percent blockage in one section of the artery and a one hundred percent blockage a little higher up in the same artery. One of the other arteries had a forty percent blockage, but that didn't seem to concern the cardiologists too much.

My next memories were of waking up in a hospital bed later that morning. I couldn't believe how much pain I felt in my chest and ribs. Apparently the paramedics had done a great job performing CPR, as I was told that ribs would break when it was done correctly. Which they had!

It hurt to breathe. Tears came to my eyes as I anticipated a sneeze coming, knowing the excruciating pain it would deliver. Every time I sneezed, it felt like someone was hitting me in the chest with a baseball bat. Fortunately, the medical staff had me on a regular dose of morphine.

The next few months would be interesting, as I knew that broken ribs took a long time to heal.

In the morning, Joanne and Rochelle, wearing huge smiles, were by my bedside welcoming me back to the land of the living. It was good to see them!

My son Brett was three hours away preparing for midterm exams in his final year of studies at the University of Alberta. He was waiting to hear the results of my surgery before making arrangements to travel home. I spoke with him on the phone to reassure him that I was fine and there was no need for him to forego his exams and travel to Calgary. I preferred that he stay safe by not driving on the slippery winter roads and instead focus on his studies. There was nothing he could do for me at this point and I felt badly that I had become a distraction to him.

Doctors and nurses visited my bedside regularly for the next few days as they checked on my status, delivered medications, and discussed my condition and prognosis with me. I rested when I could and enjoyed connecting with all the friends and relatives who visited.

When I had a chance, I attempted to process what had happened during those five minutes I was gone. Those were, without a doubt, the most important five minutes of my life—even though I was dead at the time.

TWO
DEATH-TO-LIFE EXPERIENCES

This sickness will not end in death. No, it is for
God's glory so that God's Son may be
glorified through it.
—John 11:4

I'd always wondered what death would be like... what *my* death
would be like. Would I feel pain? Would I feel a sense of peace?
Would there be angels singing as they escorted me through the
gates of heaven? Would it be scary or would I think it was the
coolest thing ever?

I've read books and seen movies in which people describe their
death experiences and claim to have seen glimpses of heaven. Some
have even claimed to see Jesus. I've heard stories of people who
claim to have returned from the dead with incredible tales of what they
saw on the other side.

To be honest, the skeptic in me always took those stories with
a grain of salt. After all, people can make up anything they want—
and they often do, in order to gain fame and fortune, or to push a
particular agenda. I've always felt more comfortable if someone could
provide proof to back up their stories and make them more believable.
Especially when it comes to something as unbelievable as coming
back from the dead!

I've only met two people who've come back from the dead. When my dad was about sixty-five, he experienced an allergic reaction to the dye the doctors used during an angioplasty procedure at the hospital. His heart stopped for about two minutes while he lay on the operating table. Fortunately, the doctors were able to revive him and he went on to live a normal life well into his nineties.

I asked him more than once whether he remembered anything from those two minutes while he was dead. He could never recall anything and had no memories of anything happening to him.

Bummer! I had really hoped to hear a life-changing revelation from someone I knew I could trust.

The other person who came back from the dead was the daughter of a pastor who served with our ministry in Mexico.

Miguel and Alicia have become good friends of ours over the years. We first met them at an underground cenote[3] in the Yucatan, where two teens on our mission team were being baptized. On this day, Miguel and Alicia stood behind our group as the baptisms were performed. They were praying and Alicia was crying tears of joy. The couple celebrated along with us the entire time.

Following the baptisms, we learned that they were pastors of a new church in the state capital, Merida. We exchanged contact information and formed a strong friendship as we partnered on many ministry endeavors through the coming years.

Not long after meeting them, we were privileged to hear the story of how they first became involved in full-time service as pastors.

Early in their marriage, while at a family function, they discovered their three-year-old daughter facedown in a swimming pool. Unresponsive, they quickly transported her to a hospital and were told that she was dead. Refusing to accept this, they rushed her to another hospital for a second opinion. This hospital, too, concurred

---

[3] A cenote is a natural sinkhole resulting from the collapse of limestone bedrock that exposes groundwater.

that she had been dead for several hours. The staff began preparing her body for the morgue.

Miguel was not a follower of Christ at the time. His mother told him that if ever he was to get serious about his relationship with God, now was the time. He prayed to God and promised that if He revived his young daughter, he would serve Him every day for the rest of his life.

Fifteen minutes later, his daughter miraculously began to breathe. However, she was in a deep coma. Although the doctors had no explanation for what had just happened, they couldn't deny the fact that she had come back to life after being clinically dead for several hours.

The doctors told Miguel and Alicia not to get their hopes up, though. Despite the fact that she was breathing again, she would likely be severely brain-damaged if she ever regained consciousness, her brain having been starved of oxygen for so long.

Five hours later, Miguel and Alicia left the hospital with a happy, healthy, perfectly normal child. The hospital staff had no explanation for what they had witnessed, but they all recognized that it was a miracle. Completely dumbfounded, the administration had Miguel and Alicia sign special documents releasing them of any future repercussions regarding their daughter's health.

Following her release, their young daughter began to describe images of heaven to her parents, including descriptions of Jesus. These were topics that had never been discussed with her, and her parents had no idea how she could have conjured them up.

They took her to a local pastor for his advice. After the pastor met with her, he too was shocked at her understanding of heaven and the descriptions she had seen. She described seeing streets of gold, brilliant colors she'd never seen before, and an amazing man who had rays of light emanating from his hands when he outstretched them.

Strangely, in the following weeks she seemed somewhat depressed. She commented to her parents that she didn't want to be there, on the earth, but rather wanted to be where the "man" was. She talked of a secret the man had told her, a secret she has yet to reveal to anyone in this life. Her desire to be with Jesus consumed her to the point that Miguel and Alicia prayed for God to remove her memories of the heavenly encounter, so she could be content here on the earth.

Today, their daughter has three beautiful children and leads a normal life. After this experience, Miguel remained true to his promise to God and became a pastor.

My only other death-to-life experience occurred while on the first mission trip that I led to Mexico in 2004. As our team prepared for a time of ministry in the local hospital in Tepic, we gathered on the sidewalk outside the main entrance. I asked the leaders of the hospital ministry to share with us what we could expect once we went inside. They proceeded to tell us that their regular teams of prayer warriors would wander the hallways and, when the Spirit prompted them, enter a room and pray for the people inside. They had seen people give their lives to God, get healed instantly, and even come back from the dead.

Whoa! I needed an explanation of that last point.

"What do you mean, you've seen people come back from the dead?" I asked incredulously.

"One day when we were walking down a hallway, we saw an entire medical team exit a room," one of the leaders explained. "We asked what had happened and were told that the patient in the room had just passed away. When we asked if it would be okay for us to go in and pray for the patient, the medical staff granted us permission but told us we'd be wasting our time. We prayed for the person and he came back to life!"

How I wished I had been there! There are so many questions I would have asked. What had he seen on the other side? What was heaven like? Had he seen Jesus?

Little did I know that I'd have my own death encounter someday—on February 3, 2019 at 3:02 a.m., to be exact.

THREE
THE MOST IMPORTANT FIVE MINUTES

As a well spent day brings happy sleep, so life
well used brings happy death.[4]
—Leonardo da Vinci

Bright lights. Streets of gold. Brilliant colors. Peaceful surroundings. Reunions with loved ones. These are the typical experiences I've heard about when people die and come back to life.

Not me. Nothing could be further from my experience.

One second I was on the couch about to get my heart checked by a paramedic and the next I was in total darkness. I remember how black it was... and I remember how anxious I felt. An overwhelming sense of anxiety consumed me!

Despite the blackness, I could see Jesus standing in front of me, off to the left, approximately ten feet away. I couldn't see His features, but I could see His silhouette as though a dim light shone behind Him. Although I couldn't see His face, I knew it was Him. I knew that I was in His presence. I could feel it. He said nothing. He didn't move. He just stood there and looked at me.

---

[4] Leonardo da Vinci, "As a well spent day…" *Goodreads*. Date of access: September 5, 2023 (https://www.goodreads.com/quotes/74114-as-a-well-spent-day-brings-happy-sleep-so-life).

There was nothing else—nothing but blackness and that heavy, overwhelming cloud of anxiety.

Then I spoke. "So… is this it? Because if it is, I'm not ready to go. I need to know you better. Please send me back." And then I kept repeating, begging, "I need to know you better! Please send me back!"

As I spoke, these words were printed in big white letters in front of my eyes.

It didn't seem like five minutes, and yet I had a sense that it was much longer than that.

To this day, I cannot explain the degree of anxiety I felt. It was frightening! It was like a dark, ominous cloud surrounding me. I didn't feel peace, like I'd heard others mention. I didn't have a sense that there was something greater awaiting me.

I felt that I wasn't ready to die. That I wasn't prepared. That I had missed the most important thing about life—getting to know Jesus intimately. I felt like it was final exam time and I had studied the wrong material! I didn't want to be there. I knew that I had lots of work to do before I made my final exit. I had so much lost time to make up. I had priorities that needed to be rearranged as quickly as possible. I needed to return to life in order to do it all!

And the only way to accomplish any of it would be to get a second chance—if I could be sent back. This is why I begged and pleaded to be sent back.

Mercifully, God allowed this to happen.

Although I didn't feel ready to die, I do remember that I had a sense of completion. I remember feeling like I had tied up my loose ends. I remember feeling a sense of relief, as I didn't have any dirty deeds that needed to be dealt with. I had ensured that my relationships with the people closest to me were healthy. This was the only thing that provided me any semblance of peace.

I will never forget the anxiety and self-condemnation I felt. How could I have been so stupid as to miss the most important part of life—getting to know Jesus intimately?

Following my death—that's a phrase I still can't get used to saying—I had vague recollections of hearing voices inform me that I had gone into cardiac arrest and was on my way to the hospital. My body had some serious healing to do, and the next several hours were lost in a fog of semi-consciousness, an operation, and then sleep and medications.

I wasn't prepared for what I was about to encounter next, once the dust settled and I was lying alone in my hospital bed.

FOUR
DREAMS DO COME TRUE

It's only when we truly know and understand that
we have a limited time on Earth—and that we
have no way of knowing when our time is up—
that we will begin to live each day to the fullest, as
if it was the only one we had.[5]
—Elisabeth Kubler-Ross

During the next few days, I received incredible medical treatment by the staff at the hospital. They did their best to stabilize me and provide the best care for my condition. And I rested when I had the chance.

During these rest periods, a recurring dream got my attention. The scenario would play out in different locations, but the exact same sequence repeated itself over and over, and the dream ended exactly the same way each time.

In the dream, I would be on my way to an arena to play ice hockey. Upon arriving with my equipment bag slung over my shoulder, I would be shocked to find that I had forgotten my hockey stick.

How can I have been so forgetful? I would wonder. *I can't play without a stick! It's such an obvious piece of equipment…*

---

[5] Elisabeth Kubler-Ross, "It's only when we truly know…" *BrainyQuote*. Date of access: September 5, 2023 (https://www.brainyquote.com/quotes/elisabeth_kublerross_661501).

Following this mental beating, I'd frantically search the arena to find, borrow, or purchase another stick so I could get into the game. No success! The pro shop would be closed and no one else would be in the arena.

This dream probably had as much impact on me as my death encounter with Jesus. I played a lot of ice hockey when I was younger and my parents always stressed the importance of mentally dressing myself before leaving home to ensure I didn't forget anything. I only had to rush home to retrieve a forgotten skate or shinpad a few times before I learned my lesson.

So I *always* checked my equipment twice. Maybe that's why I was filled with so much condemnation in the dream. A small skate or elbow pad could easily hide under the couch and be overlooked, but it would be hard to lose sight of something as large and important as a hockey stick. This would be like stepping up to the plate in baseball without a bat!

When I reflect on this dream today, I conclude that it has a direct correlation to my death encounter. The idea of being unprepared for something important makes me very uncomfortable and anxious. It always has! And when I died, I felt that I wasn't ready because I didn't know Jesus to the degree I felt was necessary.

Whether talking about my dream or my death encounter, in both situations I was not prepared.

In Matthew 25:1–13, Jesus tells a parable about ten virgins waiting for their bridegroom:

> At that time the kingdom of heaven will be like ten virgins who took their lamps and went out to meet the bridegroom. Five of them were foolish and five were wise. The foolish ones took their lamps but did not take any oil with them. The wise ones, however, took oil in jars along with their lamps. The bridegroom was a long time in coming, and they all became drowsy and fell asleep.

At midnight the cry rang out: "Here's the bridegroom! Come out to meet him!"

Then all the virgins woke up and trimmed their lamps. The foolish ones said to the wise, "Give us some of your oil; our lamps are going out."

"No," they replied, "there may not be enough for both us and you. Instead, go to those who sell oil and buy some for yourselves."

But while they were on their way to buy the oil, the bridegroom arrived. The virgins who were ready went in with him to the wedding banquet. And the door was shut.

Later the others also came. "Lord, Lord," they said, "open the door for us!"

But he replied, "Truly I tell you, I don't know you."

Therefore keep watch, because you do not know the day or the hour.

Although the purpose of this parable is to encourage people to be ready for Christ's return, I submit that it could also apply to the day when we meet Christ upon our deaths.

No doubt I was just like those foolish virgins. I knew the bridegroom was coming, that my date with death would eventually arrive, but I hadn't adequately prepared myself for that fateful day. I knew better!

I had a lot to think about.

As friends and relatives visited me in the hospital during the next week, I couldn't stop sharing what I'd experienced. I'm sure the guy in the bed next to me got tired of hearing the same story over and over, but I couldn't contain myself. As I shared my death experience and my recurring dream over and over, it served as a form of therapy, enabling me to begin the process of making sense of it all.

Hearing my closest friends' responses was interesting. One pastor was quick to provide valuable insight. He said, "Gary, you and I are very much alike. We're both doers. We like to get things done and take pride in doing a good job. We spend most of our lives doing things for God, hoping it will make Him happy."

I nodded in agreement. That's exactly what I was accustomed to doing!

"There's nothing we can do, or not do, that will make Jesus love us any more or any less than He already does," he continued. "He's not as concerned with our performance as He is with having a relationship with us. He cares about getting to know us, and us getting to know Him—not about how well we perform for Him."

Wow! That was a revelation to me. It's not that I hadn't heard the exact same thing before. In fact, I had heard it countless times. Rather, it was the timing of this revelation that mattered. For the first time, I truly understood it.

I continued to ponder this concept about not having to perform for God in order to gain His acceptance and love.

In the process, I began to think about my relationship with my own children. When I considered how I related to them, I had to ask myself: "What is it about these relationships that I really desire?"

When my children were younger, would I have loved them any more or less if they came home from school with straight As or straight Fs? Of course not! Their performance would not have affected the degree to which I loved them.

The answer to my fundamental question was that I was most concerned about having a close relationship with them. Spending time with them. Doing things with them. Conversing with them. Getting to know them better.

Our Heavenly Father is no different. He's concerned more with having a relationship with us than with how well we do things for Him. He wants to spend time with us. He wants to talk with us, and for us to talk to Him. He wants our relationship to grow and flourish!

Sadly, I had heard all this before, countless times and in many forms. I grew up in a Christian home. My parents became missionaries shortly after they were married. I invited Christ to come into my life when I was five. I went to a Christian high school and a Christian university. I served as a missionary for many years and eventually started my own ministry.

But none of this mattered, because I never really understood what it meant to have a personal relationship with my Creator. Sure, I understood it from a *head-knowledge* perspective, but I should have been focusing on understanding it from a *heart* perspective.

To have a relationship with my wife and kids, I know that it's necessary to do certain things. Spending time with them is important if I want to develop intimacy with them. Talking to them and listening to them is a necessary part of developing these relationships.

However, these relationships won't go anywhere if I don't apply what I know. I need to invest myself in the relationships. If I want to see these relationships flourish, if I want to develop true intimacy, it will take time, effort, and commitment. All the head-knowledge in the world won't help me improve my relationship with my family if I don't take action and apply it.

Our relationship with our Lord and Savior is no different. Too many of us think we have it all figured out. We think we know how to have a close relationship with God, but we never get to the point of actually making it happen. How pointless! How tragic!

That's exactly where I was. I had all the head-knowledge I needed but had failed to put it into practice. I was too focused on doing things for the betterment of the Kingdom when I should have been focused on developing a deeper relationship with Jesus. Sure, there were seasons when I felt close to Him, but those seasons, if I'm completely honest, were few and far between. There were periods of time, often several months long, when I studied the Bible, led small groups, and tried to get deeper in my faith. These were great times, but they didn't occur consistently. There seemed to be a disconnect. I was going through the motions, playing the part.

So how do we get to the point in our lives at which, as the psalmist says, having a close relationship with God becomes crucial to our survival?

As the deer pants for streams of water, so my soul pants
for you, my God. My soul thirsts for God, for the living God.
When can I go and meet with God? (Psalm 42:1–2)

That's where I wanted to be. That's what I wanted my relationship
with God to be like. That became my new goal, what I had been
missing for so many years.

My journey to implement *The Most Important Lesson* began on
February 3, 2019, when my heart stopped and I was clinically dead for
five minutes. The rest of this book will illuminate the lightbulb moments
that have propelled me to get to know Jesus intimately. Some of these
revelations may seem trivial, but my goal is simply to share my story in
the hopes that it may resonate with others.

Although I heard some important lessons throughout my life, my
personal history provides ample proof that some of them didn't sink
in as they should have. I ignored warning signs and misplaced my
priorities.

I should add that this book is the result of a conversation I had
with God roughly a month after I died. During that conversation in
the middle of the night, God told me to write the book and tell my
story. He told me that He would give me the words. He countered
every argument I put forth and eventually won the battle. I knew that I
needed to put my trust in Him, so I conceded. Soon after, I began the
process of organizing my thoughts.

But what about these so-called "conversations" with God? This
may seem like a very strange concept. The truth is that God speaks
to His people in a variety of ways. After all, He is God and can do
anything He wants! Allow me to touch on just a few of the ways
through which God communicates with us.

To some, God actually speaks in an audible voice. Adam and
Eve heard God's voice in the Garden of Eden (Genesis 3:8). He spoke
audibly to Moses from the burning bush (Exodus 3:4–6) and to all
of Israel from Mount Sinai (Exodus 20:1–22). In the New Testament,

He endorsed Jesus at His baptism and the transfiguration with a literal voice. Following Jesus's death and resurrection, Saul and his companions then saw Him in a blinding light and heard His voice (Acts 9:3–7).

God sometimes speaks to us through His still, small voice. A biblical example can be seen when Elijah camped in a cave on Mount Sinai. He heard God speak to him in a still, small voice, which is also translated as *"a gentle whisper"* (1 Kings 19:12).

At other times, God speaks through visions and dreams: *"I will pour out my Spirit on all people. Your sons and daughters will prophesy, your young men will see visions, your old men will dream dreams"* (Acts 2:17). A vision is an inspired appearance, something one can see either literally with their eyes or spiritually with their minds or spirits. A dream is something seen in one's sleep, or something a person imagines themself doing. God can insert images and ideas into our minds whether or not we are conscious of it.

For example, God gave me a vision of what our current ministry, C-Quest, would look like. This vision launched my wife and me on our biggest journey of faith with Him. He has continued to sustain and direct us in this ministry for many years.

When I hear from God, it usually happens through His still, small voice, or through visions. At times I have experienced such strong dialogue with Him that it is similar to having a normal conversation, although I have never heard Him speak audibly. There is no better way to explain this other than to say that I simply *know* God is talking to me, just like I *knew* that I was in His presence when I died.

I hope this helps to provide you with a clearer picture of what I mean when I write about hearing from God.

I strongly believe that I have been hearing from God more frequently and clearly in recent years, since my cardiac arrest. I am making a greater effort now to listen to Him. It's hard to hear someone if you're not listening. It will be very difficult to hear God speak if our lives are filled with too much noise—too many distractions and diversions.

It also takes effort. Effort to quiet ourselves so we can spend time simply listening. A great place to start is to ask God what He might want to say to us. It's so easy to fill our lives with noise. It can become addictive to turn on the noise—the television, the music, the computer—to provide ourselves with a sense of companionship. Doing so can interfere with our ability to hear God speak. Before my death encounter, I was notorious for filling my life with noise.

Now I make an effort to listen more intently and ask Him what He wants to say. Sometimes I don't hear anything. Maybe this is why God tends to talk to me in the middle of the night. There's not much to distract me at that time, meaning that I can solely focus on Him. I can be still and hear His voice.

It is commonly known that animals can instantly recognize the voice of a familiar and trusted person. Sheep recognize the voice of their shepherd. They follow him (or her). The shepherd protects his flock and would give his life for them.

Jesus said, *"My sheep listen to my voice"* (John 10:27). The Greek word used here for listen is *ginō´skō*, which refers to our knowing God or Christ in an intimate, spiritual sense, and in turn being known by them.[6] As the Good Shepherd, Jesus knows His own intimately, and they in turn know Him intimately.

In John 10:27, Jesus confirms that His sheep will keep hearing His voice, that He Himself will keep knowing them, and that they will keep following Him.

Like any skill, the more we practice good listening habits with God, the better we'll be able to hear from Him.

---

[6] *The Logos of Agape*, "Ginosko, a Greek Word Study." July 26, 2018 (https://thelogosofagape.wordpress.com/2018/07/26/ginosko-a-greek-word-study).

FIVE

DEATH IS UNPREDICTABLE YET INEVITABLE

It matters not how a man dies, but how he lives.[7]
—Samuel Johnson

No one knows exactly when they're going to die. But it will happen to each of us some day. Guaranteed!

I'm always amazed at the videos and photos I find online of people seeming to challenge death. They do crazy things like hang from the edge of skyscrapers by one hand while taking a selfie with the other. Rock-climbers scale tall mountains, or buildings, using only their fingertips to grip.

The list could go on. I could never wrap my head around this desire to constantly flirt with death. Why do some people consciously put their lives in such precarious situations when a slight miscalculation or slip of the fingers would mean the end? Is any adrenaline rush, photo, or video worth that?

Other times we flirt with death and never know it.

Several years ago, while working for a mission organization that trained youth to use the arts to share the gospel overseas, I had the pleasure of escorting a team to the Philippines. I stayed for a few days to ensure they were acclimated and off to a good start in their ministry.

---

[7] Samuel Johnson, "It matter not how a man dies…" *AZ Quotes*. Date of access: September 5, 2023 (https://www.azquotes.com/quote/148722).

I always look for good scuba diving opportunities when I travel overseas. With so many tropical islands to explore, I knew that the Philippines had some of the world's best locations, including spectacular reefs with whale sharks, manta rays, and every imaginable form of tropical fish. It's a paradise for divers and snorkelers.

On my day off, we traveled to an area known for its excellent scuba diving and I arranged for a local guide to take me diving. This is probably the best day I've ever spent underwater. The variety and quantity of marine life was unlike anything I had ever experienced.

On one of two dives that day, I had the pleasure of being engulfed in a large school of jackfish. They ignored my presence and for several minutes I was surrounded by thousands of these foot-long white fish as they swam by. All I could see were jackfish in every direction.

After a while, they simply moved on—to look for more food, I presume, since that is how I think fish spend most of their days. What a life!

At one point, I found myself in an area with rocky patches of seabed interspersed with sand. In my search for something interesting to see, I positioned my body into a neutrally buoyant horizontal position, lowering myself just a few inches above the bottom.

A few seconds later, my attention was caught by the distinct sound of metallic rapping. Looking around to find the source of the sound, I saw my guide frantically tapping his pointing stick against a rock. Once he had my attention, he gestured to a fish positioned just a few centimeters from my stomach. It was camouflaged so well and I hadn't noticed it against the rocks. He motioned for me to slowly pull away—and I promptly obeyed. He breathed a huge sigh of relief once I was a safe distance from the fish.

Not knowing the danger I had inadvertently put myself in, I carried on with the dive as though nothing had happened.

When we eventually surfaced, my guide took no time in informing me that I had nearly set myself on top of a stonefish, the most venomous fish in the sea. He told me that had I been stung by one of its poisonous spines, I would not have made it to the surface alive.

To satisfy my curiosity, I later did some research on the stonefish, and he was correct. Reports vary on exactly how life-threatening their venom is, but it is agreed by all experts that a person, if stung, would need immediate medical attention. That day, we had been a long way from "immediate medical attention."

Thanks to the attentiveness and keen eyes of my guide, I lived to dive another day.

Near-death experiences like this one remind me of the fragility and unpredictability of life. Any one of us can die at any minute.

I was reminded of this again on a summer day in 1999 when I read the front page news story of John F. Kennedy Jr., who died while flying his own plane to his cousin's wedding. The plane crashed into the ocean, carrying John, his wife Carolyn, and his sister-in-law Lauren Bessette. At the age of thirty-eight, John was a handsome lawyer, journalist, and magazine publisher. He and his family were considered American royalty, and he was no doubt destined for a career in politics, just like his famous presidential father.

For some reason, this particular death impacted me. I kept the clipping of that news story.

On April 6, 2018, the driver of a semi-trailer failed to yield at a flashing stop sign at the intersection of two highways in a remote area of the Canadian prairies. The semi was travelling at a speed of approximately one hundred kilometres per hour (sixty miles per hour). Consequently, sixteen people were killed and thirteen severely injured when the semi struck a northbound bus. Most of the dead and injured were young hockey players from the Humboldt Broncos, a team in the Saskatchewan Junior Hockey League (SJHL). These young men, between the ages of sixteen and twenty-one, were in the prime of their lives, enjoying a sport they loved, when they were tragically and unexpectedly taken from us. None of these players had woken up that morning expecting their lives to be cut short.

Whenever I see a person, often a celebrity or athlete, die prematurely at the height of their career and family life, it serves to remind me that life is fragile. The end cannot be predicted.

So what can we learn from this? What do we do with the time we're given, not knowing when it will end? That's what this book is about.

But for now, let's summarize this lesson by understanding that life is short and precious—and death is unpredictable and inevitable.

I think most of us would agree that we'd like to get the most out of our time here on the earth.

I've always been intrigued by the thoughts and final words of people on their deathbeds, knowing that the end is near. As they reflect on their lives, their words often reflect what is truly meaningful to them.

David Cassidy, an actor and recording star, passed away on November 21, 2017 of liver disease. He started life as a teen idol and ended it as an alcoholic, literally drinking himself to a premature death.

"You know, I did it to myself, man," Cassidy said. "I did it to myself to cover up the sadness and the emptiness."

Shortly after his death, I remember reading an article in which his daughter said that his final words were "So much wasted time." To live your whole life and at the end feel like it has been a big waste of time… how sad!

In contrast, Jesus said in John 10:10, *"I have come that they may have life, and have it to the full."* What does that mean, to live life to the full? Does this mean that if I believe in Jesus and choose to follow Him, He will make my life into one big happy vacation? That all my problems will be solved? That my car will never get a flat tire? That He will bless me with untold riches and perfect health for the rest of my days?

No.

Unfortunately, many false teachers out there will tell you the opposite. Run from them! This is not what the Bible, God's Word, teaches. Jesus said, *"I have told you these things, so that in me you may have peace. In this world you will have trouble. But take heart! I have overcome the world"* (John 16:33).

The only way to live a fully abundant life is to develop an intimate relationship with Jesus and then experience all that He has to offer. This is the most important lesson any of us will ever learn!

Developing an intimate relationship with Jesus is about more than simply acknowledging that there is a God. James 2:19 tells us, *"You believe that there is one God. Good! Even the demons believe that— and shudder."* Too many people think that because they believe there is a God, they've covered their bases, saved themselves from hell, and can go on living their lives as they please.

This is not what God teaches in the Bible. We must live our lives in obedience to Him, loving Him and others as ourselves.

Some people think that because they do Christian things—like go to church, give to charities, and respect those around them—they are good Christians. Jesus makes it very clear that these people are deceiving themselves and living with a false sense of security.

> Not everyone who says to me, "Lord, Lord," will enter the kingdom of heaven, but only the one who does the will of my Father who is in heaven. Many will say to me on that day, "Lord, Lord, did we not prophesy in your name and in your name drive out demons and in your name perform many miracles?" Then I will tell them plainly, "I never knew you. Away from me, you evildoers!" (Matthew 7:21–23)

God knows our hearts. We can put on a Christian show outwardly, making ourselves look good to those around us, but that means nothing to God. He cares about what's in our hearts, what our true motivations are, what our real desires are. He knows whether we're serious about having a relationship with Him.

...for the Lord searches every heart and understands every desire and every thought. If you seek him, he will be found by you; but if you forsake him, he will reject you forever. (1 Chronicles 28:9)

The big question then is this: how do we develop intimacy with Jesus Christ and come to know Him like He wants us to? Please continue reading with an open heart and mind. May Jesus reveal Himself to you and begin to shape your heart into one patterned after His.

In the meantime, don't text while driving, take your selfies with both feet on the ground, and avoid stonefish at all costs!

SIX

MEETING SOMEONE FAMOUS

Life is beautiful not because of the things we see
or the things we do. Life is beautiful because of
the people we meet.[8]

—Simon Sinek

Have you ever met someone famous? Maybe you bumped into a movie star in a coffee shop, or sat beside a celebrity on an airplane. Maybe you walked by someone famous on a beach while on vacation, or shook hands with them in the lobby following one of their performances.

Why is it that we put so much value in meeting someone we consider to be famous?

During the summer months when I was in high school, I worked for a trucking company in Red Deer, Alberta, delivering chemicals and drilling mud to oil rigs. It was unusual to work on a Sunday, but one day I was called into the shop along with a co-worker to arrange for an emergency shipment. We were just wrapping up our job when a large, brightly colored eighteen-wheeler pulled into our yard. The driver got out along with a man who looked strangely familiar.

---

[8] Simon Sinek, "Life is beautiful not because…" *Goodreads*. Date of access: September 5, 2023 (https://www.goodreads.com/quotes/10499668-life-is-beautiful-not-because-of-the-things-we-see).

It was Evel Knievel!

For those of you who don't know, Evel Knievel was one of the world's greatest stunt performers. He was famous for attempting more than seventy-five death-defying ramp-to-ramp motorcycle jumps in the 1960s and 1970s. The key word there is *attempting*. In reality, he became more famous for his bone-crushing crashes than successful jumps.

On December 31, 1967, he unsuccessfully attempted to jump his motorcycle over the fountains at Caesars Palace in Las Vegas. He landed short of his landing ramp, and as a result suffered a crushed pelvis and femur, fractures to his hip, wrist, and both ankles, and a concussion that kept him in the hospital for an extended period of time. At the time, the Caesars Palace crash was Knievel's longest attempted motorcycle jump at forty-three meters (141 feet). This jump, although unsuccessful, launched him to stardom.

On September 8, 1974, he attempted to jump the Snake River Canyon in Idaho in his steam-powered, rocket-propelled Skycycle X-2. His parachute deployed early during the launch, but he still made it across the canyon successfully.

Upon touchdown, however, the prevailing winds caught the parachute and dragged the Skycycle X-2 to the bottom of the canyon, narrowly missing the river by just a few feet. His safety harness had malfunctioned and he admitted afterwards that he would have surely drowned had he landed in the river.

On May 26, 1975, in front of ninety thousand people at Wembley Stadium in London, England, Knievel broke his pelvis when he crashed while trying to land a jump over thirteen London buses.

You get the point. This guy was awesome!

On the day I met him, he was on his way from the United States to perform a show in Edmonton and desperately needed fuel for his rig. Back in the late 1970s, gas stations weren't open on Sundays in Alberta and he and his driver hadn't known this upon crossing the border a few hours earlier. When they couldn't find an open gas station, they figured that maybe a trucking company in the industrial section of town would have fuel.

They were in luck. We did.

While we filled his rig with diesel, he gave us a guided tour of his semitrailer. It was like a museum of memories in tribute to his career. It contained the Skycycle X-2, other motorcycles he'd used, and some of his famous red, white, and blue leather jumpsuits. We were in awe!

Before he left, his driver paid us for the fuel and he gave each of us an autographed photo and a vinyl record album containing his biography. As his fancy rig slowly pulled out of our yard, I remember waving and wondering if what I'd just experienced had really happened.

I had one more quick brush with fame later in life. While studying aviation at a university in British Columbia just out of high school, I played hockey for the school team. Each spring break we traveled for games in other provinces, as well as in the U.S.

One year we made the trip to southern California to play the major universities. On a day off, a friend who lived in the Los Angeles area offered to take a few of us sightseeing. We gladly accepted and I hopped in his car with a few of my teammates.

While driving down Rodeo Drive in Beverly Hills, we were amazed at the designer boutiques and opulence oozing from every storefront. At a stoplight, we pulled up behind a white Rolls Royce with a customized license plate that read ZZG. I wondered if it could possibly belong to the famous actress, Zsa Zsa Gabor.

When the light turned green, I asked my friend to quickly pull up beside the car so we could see who was driving. Sure enough, it was her, driving her own car—without tinted windows! So much for flying under the radar.

We stayed in the lane beside her for a few seconds, took some quick photos, and then she looked over at us and hit the brakes. We weren't prepared for her sudden change in speed and inadvertently ended up in front of her as she attempted to ditch us. We took the next right turn and pulled over to the curb. She proceeded straight. We then backed up and fell in behind her again.

Hey, we were dumb kids looking for some excitement, not really thinking about the trauma we were undoubtedly causing this poor lady.

We followed as she entered the exclusive neighborhood of Bel Air. Winding through the huge mansions and exquisitely groomed foliage, we were giddy with excitement, wondering how this adventure might end. Maybe she would invite us in for afternoon tea!

Eventually her car pulled up in front of a beautiful mansion with some large wrought-iron gates. The gates slowly opened and she drove in. Once she had safely entered, a large black sedan with tinted windows pulled out to the entrance and sat there.

This was our exit cue! We took it as a warning and quickly drove away.

It took a while for the smiles to leave our faces and our hearts to stop pounding. We had some precious photos to remember our adventure and a fun story to share with our teammates.

I apologize to Ms. Gabor for our youthful indiscretion.

There's no doubt about it: meeting someone famous is thrilling! Is it life-changing? Probably not. But these experiences do serve to add excitement to our lives while also producing some good stories.

What kind of person could change our lives for the better just by meeting them? The Bible is filled with the stories of people whose lives were changed by meeting Jesus. One of my favorites is the story of Zacchaeus.

Zacchaeus was a tax collector and was considered one of the most unpopular people in Israel at the time. To finance their great world empire, the Romans levied taxes against the Jews and all other nations under their control. In Israel, tax collectors were Jews who worked for the Roman government. They were considered traitors, making themselves rich by extorting their fellow Jews.

Zacchaeus was no different. He was despised by his countrymen.

One day while Jesus passed through the town where Zacchaeus lived, a crowd of people came out to meet Him. By this time, He had become very popular. Zacchaeus tried to squeeze through the crowd to get a look at Jesus, but because of his small stature and unpopularity no one would let him through. He decided to run ahead and climb a tree to get a better view.

When Jesus walked by this tree, He looked up into the branches and said, *"Zacchaeus, come down immediately. I must stay at your house today"* (Luke 19:5).

Whoa! The people couldn't believe what they had just seen and heard. They were blown away by the fact that Jesus would acknowledge someone like Zacchaeus, let alone ask to go to his home!

After he met Jesus, probably over a meal, Zacchaeus realized that his life needed straightening out. He said to Jesus, *"Look, Lord! Here and now I give half of my possessions to the poor, and if I have cheated anybody out of anything, I will pay back four times the amount"* (Luke 19:8).

For a guy whose priority in life had been getting rich, this was quite the change! After meeting Jesus, this priority paled in comparison to following Him and doing what was right.

Jesus replied, *"Today salvation has come to this house…"* (Luke 19:9)

This is a great example of the life-changing transformation that can occur in people's lives when they meet Jesus. Getting to know Jesus intimately is the key to salvation and eternal life. He is the most important person to have ever walked the earth and He wants to have a relationship with you!

SEVEN

IT TAKES A LEAP OF FAITH
TO GET ANYWHERE

Faith is the strength by which a shattered world
shall emerge into the light.[9]
—Helen Keller

I've always been somewhat of an adrenaline junkie. I can remember
doing things as a child that seemed like good ideas at the time. They
often turned into regretful experiences. My parents told stories of me
doing stupid things like getting my head stuck between the metal bars
on the stairway of the Legislature and riding my tricycle almost eight
kilometres (five miles) outside of town to see some family friends when
I was four years old.

One of my all-time bucket-list goals was to try skydiving. I had
often imagined what it would be like to freefall through the air and float
gently down to earth like a dying leaf from a tree in autumn.

Okay, maybe not the best analogy.

This had to be one of the ultimate adrenaline rushes, I
thought. The experience would be euphoric, undoubtedly! I'd seen
countless videos of skydivers masterfully controlling their bodies and

[9] Helen Keller, "Faith is the strength…" *BiblePortal*. Date of access: September 5, 2023 (https://bibleportal.com/bible-quote/faith-strength-light-faith-is-the-strength-by-which-a-shattered-world-shall-emerge-into-the-light).

conducting amazing feats of athleticism and acrobatics in the sky, piloting their bodies with pinpoint accuracy to their landing zones and then gracefully touching down with huge smiles on their faces. I was destined for this!

In my early thirties, Joanne finally gave in to my petitions. For my birthday one year, she gave me a gift certificate for a skydiving experience. I soon discovered how easy it is to *talk* about how much fun it would be to conquer something daring and death-defying. But my dream, or perhaps my nightmare, was now becoming reality!

Since my birthday was in February, I had to wait until spring to redeem the gift certificate. Midwinter isn't the best time to skydive in Canada; the temperatures can plummet to face-numbing digits, and they're even colder at higher altitudes.

After waiting a few months for the temperature to rise, the day finally arrived and I reserved a spot for my first jump.

There are two ways to skydive for first-timers like myself. Successfully and unsuccessfully would be one answer, but not the one I'm referring to.

The first way, one I learned about after the fact, was that you could go "tandem." This is where the novice attaches himself to the front of an experienced skydiving instructor and they jump from the airplane joined together as one. Soaring through the air, the instructor whispers reassurances into the ear of the novice while they float nonchalantly to earth. This would be the ultimate stress-free first dive experience.

The other way is to jump from the plane solo as you look up to see your instructor fly away in the airplane you just exited. This method involves the instructor pulling the novice's "pilot chute" from the knapsack that contains the parachute and then throwing it into the air so that it, hopefully, catches the air and then pulls out the main canopy. If all goes well and the canopy opens like it should, the novice is then given instructions, through a one-way radio attached to his chest, by another instructor on the ground who directs him to the landing zone. The novice is taught in ground school which toggles to pull on the parachute in order to steer to the drop zone.

This is the method I chose for my first skydive.

It was a cool Monday morning when I arrived at the skydive center located about an hour northeast of Calgary. I entered the building that contained the ground school and was surprised to see the room full of about twenty young British soldiers. I hadn't been aware that this particular skydiving school was responsible for training the entire British military in how to skydive. I was impressed.

The teacher stepped up to the front of the classroom and informed us that before training commenced we would be required to watch a video. It was a legal requirement. In the video, a lawyer explained that it was our choice to be there and no one was forcing us to jump out of a perfectly good airplane. He further explained that we would soon be handed some legal documents to sign, releasing the skydiving school from any liability should something go wrong.

I get nervous signing any legal document, but this one was a doozy! Nevertheless, I signed the document, because I saw everyone else doing so. I figured it would be pointless to resist.

I had given myself a pep talk during the drive out and convinced myself that the only way I would return home was as a successful skydiver. If signing this document meant I had cleared the first obstacle, then full speed ahead!

Following the signing, we sat through a morning of instruction. This mostly consisted of learning routines and procedures for what to do if something went wrong. Near the end of the morning, we were escorted out to the fuselage of a small aircraft positioned in the middle of the training compound. I wondered if this plane had been parked here after a previous trip that hadn't gone as planned!

We practiced getting in and out of the aircraft. Nothing to it. We were a whole twelve inches off the ground, so it wasn't the least bit scary.

Meanwhile, other young British soldiers were coming in from their morning jumps. The landing zone wasn't far away and it was entertaining to watch some of their landings as we waited for our turn. The winds were picking up quite a bit and this appeared to cause some difficulty for the notice divers. In fact, before we were finished with our simulated airplane exits, one of the more advanced students, during his descent, floated into the side of a nearby airplane hangar. Oops! I figured this was just another day in the life of a soldier and paid it little attention.

Much to my dismay, once we had completed our practiced fuselage exits, we were told by our instructor that it was too windy for us to proceed with our first jump. Disappointed but somewhat relieved, I drove home and had to wait until Wednesday to return and complete my jump. The rest of my classmates were scheduled to go up for their first jumps on Tuesday, but unfortunately I had a prior commitment that day.

When Wednesday morning rolled around, I returned to the skydive center, once again pep-talking myself all the way. Upon my arrival, I was greeted by a young, friendly soldier who recognized me from our ground school class two days earlier.

As we walked to the hangar to get into our skydiving suits and pick up our parachutes, he said, "So did you hear about the guy yesterday?"

"What do you mean?"

"One of our guys plummeted!"

"What do you mean, he plummeted?"

"One of our guys panicked when he got out onto the wing," he continued. "He wouldn't let go of the strut—and when he finally did he only released his right hand. This caused him to spin around. When he did let go of the airplane, the pilot chute got wrapped around his arm."

"What happened next?" My voice got higher, my curiosity piqued.

"We watched as he plummeted," the soldier nonchalantly explained as if he were ordering a decaf latte at the local coffee shop.

"We watched him fall. Just before he hit the ground, he finally pulled his reserve chute. But it didn't open all the way. Not enough time."

I had to ask. "Soooo… is he dead?"

"No, he's in the hospital with almost every bone in his body broken. He landed about two kilometers from the drop zone. Crushed his legs and his spine. But he's still alive. For now."

We continued walking up to the hangar.

"You're gonna crap your pants!" the guy added.

No kidding! Of course, his actual language was a little more colorful than what I've described here.

All the way out to the hangar, which seemed like a million miles away, he kept repeating it: "You're gonna crap your pants!"

I must have heard it a dozen times enroute. I guess that was his way of reassuring me, or maybe he was trying to justify the state of his own shorts at the time.

Upon our arrival at the hangar, everyone got busy locating a parachute that had already been packed. As we suited up, I felt at a distinct disadvantage. The day prior, my fellow ground school compatriots had gone through the drill and accomplished their first two dives. This was all routine to them by now. I tried my best to look like I knew what I was doing and imitated them. Arms go here, this strap connects there, etc.

Once we were in our suits, we lined up in preparation to board the airplane—with me at the front of the line. This was not good! I had no one to mimic if I was at the front. I soon figured out that they wanted me to board first in order to jump last, something they did for the greenest divers. In the event that I chickened out and refused to leave the plane, the other divers wouldn't have to awkwardly crawl over me in order to exit the airplane.

Apparently this is a frequent occurrence.

Luckily, my new buddy was right behind me. Close enough to continue his motivational pep talk in my ear: "You're gonna crap your pants!" Somehow I found comfort in this. Knowing that I probably wasn't the most fearful diver aboard gave me a strange sense of courage.

Since the other divers already had two successful dives under their belts, they had already reached the next stage towards becoming certified freefall skydivers. This stage involved completing three successful "paper pulls." They each entered the airplane with a page of newsprint rolled tightly into a tube. This tube was stuffed into a strap that was attached to one of their thighs. After exiting the plane, their mission was to reach down, grab the tube, and simply throw it into the air. This would indicate to the instructor that they had the clarity of mind to eventually pull their own ripcord and release their parachute.

We lined up on our knees in a horseshoe pattern inside the airplane. This positioned me right by the door, just behind the instructor and the next jumper. The instructor warned me that the door would open when we reached the appropriate altitude, creating a lot of noise and wind. Due to my previous experience flying small planes, this was no surprise to me. I accepted the warning with relative calm.

What did surprise me, however, was when the wind from the open door sucked out every single rolled-up paper tube from the divers' thighs. I think I may have chuckled.

The airplane eventually leveled off and I watched as the instructor had the first diver bend over so he could remove the pilot chute from his backpack. This is what catches the air and pulls out the main canopy. Next, the diver reached through the open door and took hold of the strut of the wing, just as we had practiced in ground school. He then inched his feet out onto a thin metal bar extending twenty-four inches from the aircraft.

Once in place outside the airplane, the diver looked at the instructor, got the go-ahead to release his grip from the strut, and fell away while forming an "X" with his body. Roughly five seconds after beginning his fall, the pilot chute pulled out the main canopy and the diver reached up, grabbed the toggles on each side of the canopy, and began steering himself towards the drop zone.

One by one I watched as each diver exited the plane successfully. My anticipation and anxiety increased a bit more with each jump, knowing that my turn was getting closer.

With only one jumper left in front of me, I watched more intently. My buddy was about to jump. He grabbed the strut and worked his feet carefully out onto the metal bar. He looked at the instructor and was given the go-ahead to release.

He froze.

Over the wind and engine noise, the instructor continued yelling at him to release, but the guy just stood there with a look of terror on his face, gripping the wing strut with all his might.

This got awkward really quick!

I remember thinking to myself that this guy already had at least two dives under his belt. Why was he freaking out now?

We waited. For what seemed like an eternity.

I'm sure it was no more than thirty seconds in real time, but it seemed much longer. Finally, with the instructor yelling at him, I watched as the man closed his eyes tightly and released his death grip on the strut. Approximately five seconds later, his main canopy opened and he began his graceful descent.

The instructor turned to me and motioned me to move forward and bend over so he could remove the pilot chute from my pack. My mind was running a million miles an hour. I looked up, positioned my hands on the strut, and carefully placed my right foot onto the bar.

It's all going as planned, I kept telling myself. *I've been in countless small airplanes and this is no big deal.*

The gravity of the situation never really hit me until I looked down and saw my feet standing on this tiny metal bar. There was *nothing* between my feet and the ground 3,500 feet below. I will never forget that moment! The rush of wind and engine noise was deafening and I was hanging onto the outside of the plane midflight. I kept reminding myself of the promise I had made to myself that I would only return to the ground by parachute. I could do this!

I looked at the instructor just like I was taught to do. He had seemed so safe and comfortable inside the airplane! Now he made direct eye contact and gave me the go-ahead to release. I took a deep breath and let go.

As quickly as possible, I formed the "X" position. This was no time to experiment with other letters of the alphabet!

One one thousand. Two one thousand. Three one thousand. Four one thousand. Five one thousand.

This was the moment when my main canopy should open, according to what I had learned in ground school. The rush of wind was all I could hear, but then I remembered hearing something I hadn't heard before. Looking up, I saw the glorious unfolding of my main canopy as it was pulled from my pack. It formed just above my head, right where it was supposed to be. I think I may have heard violins play and angels sing at that moment!

Now that the pressure was off, I could relax and enjoy the ride. I was going to live after all! I reached up, grabbed the toggles, and tried some turns. This was pretty cool! I could see other divers below at various stages of their descent. I could now also hear a voice coming from the radio attached to my chest.

The voice gave instructions to each diver by number. "Diver number five, turn ninety degrees right and hold course. Diver number six, you're doing fine. Diver number seven, turn forty-five degrees left. Diver number eight, turn one hundred eighty degrees. Diver number five, turn forty-five degrees left. Diver number six, forty-five degrees right and hold. Diver number eight, turn ninety degrees right. Diver number five, hold course… aaannndddd… flare. Congratulations!"

This narrative continued through my entire descent.

About halfway down, I realized that I had been following the instructions being given to one of the other divers. It finally dawned on me that I was diver number eight.

From then on, I quickly obeyed the instructions and was successfully brought closer and closer to the drop zone.

"Diver number eight, correct course forty-five degrees left and hold. Aaannnnndddddd… flare, flare, flare!"

With that, I turned the small amount needed in order to line myself up with my landing site. I thrust both of my hands down in order to flare the parachute so I could touch down at a slower speed. There was quite a bit of wind that day, so my landing wasn't quite as picture-perfect as I would have liked. My feet touched the ground with a thud and the wind carried my canopy to the left, causing me to topple over. But I was on the ground safely!

I quickly got up and began to gather my canopy and clear the drop zone, not that it mattered since I was the last jumper to land.

I had made it! I was alive! No smell of soiled shorts! The euphoria and feeling of accomplishment was incredible. Another check off the old bucket list!

It's been many years now since that first skydiving experience. I've often used this story to talk to others about conquering fear, setting goals, and taking risks. But the greatest lesson I take from this experience is that without faith, we accomplish very little in life. In order to skydive successfully, I was required to put faith in my instructors, in the guy who had packed my parachute, in the pilot who flew the airplane, and most importantly in the parachute itself.

We all exercise faith in order to live our lives. We have faith that the water we drink and the food we eat won't make us sick. We have faith that the drivers coming towards us will stay in their lanes and not cross into ours. We have faith that the roof over our heads will stay strong and upright through the night as we sleep below. We have faith that the sun won't blow up today.

Faith is a choice we make, sometimes consciously and sometimes without realizing it. Without faith, we would be paralyzed by fear. Maybe this is why God talks so much about fear and faith in the Bible. He tells us that we are not to live our lives in fear, and that in order to please Him we need to exercise our faith—in Him.

> And without faith it is impossible to please God, because anyone who comes to him must believe that he exists and that he rewards those who earnestly seek him. (Hebrews 11:6)

We all have faith in something or someone. Whether we're devout followers of Jesus Christ or claim to be atheists, we exercise faith. The concept of faith is understood to involve believing in something without a certain kind or amount of evidence—the kind or amount that would give us certain proof.

The atheist exercises an immense amount of faith in choosing to believe that everything seen and experienced came about by accident. They believe that everything was created from nothing, that what we perceive as having been designed actually resulted from chaos—totally contradicting the second law of thermodynamics. They trust in science yet deny it at the same time!

Faith is a fundamental aspect of the human condition. All relationships require faith. Because we are incapable of fully knowing other people and God, to some degree faith (trust) is an integral ingredient in all of our relationships.

This question is answered well by the writers of Got Questions, a website devoted to tackling questions about faith and the Bible:

> If we cannot know our fellow finite human beings fully, how can we expect to fully know an infinite God? Even if He should desire to fully reveal Himself, it is impossible for us to fully know Him. It is like trying to pour the ocean (seemingly infinite in quantity) into a quart-measuring jar (finite)… impossible! Nonetheless, even as we can have meaningful relationships with others that we have grown to trust because of our knowledge of them and of their character, so

God has revealed enough about Himself through His creation (Romans 1:18–21), through His written Word, the Bible (2 Timothy 3:16–17; 2 Peter 1:16–21), and through His Son (John 14:9), that we can enter into a meaningful relationship with Him. But this is only possible when the barrier of one's sin has been removed by trusting in Christ's person and work on the cross as payment for one's sin. This is necessary because, as it is impossible for both light and darkness to dwell together, so it is impossible for a holy God to have fellowship with sinful man unless his sin has been paid for and removed. Jesus Christ, the sinless Son of God, died on the cross to take our punishment and change us so that the one who believes on Him can become a child of God and live eternally in His presence (John 1:12; 2 Corinthians 5:21; 2 Peter 3:18; Romans 3:10–26).[10]

As you can clearly see, the decision to take a step of faith and build a relationship with our Creator and His Son Jesus Christ is foundational to learning *The Most Important Lesson.*

Without faith, it would be equivalent to jumping out of an airplane and flapping our arms in order to save ourselves. God has given us a parachute to save us. His name is Jesus. He was sent by God to save us from spending eternity separated from Him in hell.

Trust the parachute!

---

[10] "Why Does God Require Faith?" *God Questions.org.* Date of access: July 26, 2023 (https://www.gotquestions.org/God-require-faith.html).

EIGHT
TREASURE HUNTING

He is no fool who gives what he cannot keep to
gain that which he cannot lose.[11]
—Jim Elliot

I've always wondered what it would feel like to find a treasure. Whether
it's buried, sunken, or purchased in a garage sale, the thought of
finding something extremely valuable, even life-changing, never fails
to capture my interest.

Then one day I found it.

I taught school for fifteen years, and for most of my teaching
career I taught sixth-graders. I loved this age because the kids were
always eager to engage in topics that interested them. I discovered
that I had the most success when I could immerse my students in an
experience and make a topic as relevant as possible. If I could make
school not feel like "school," learning became fun for everyone—
including me.

One year, I developed a unit on treasure. As a class we read books
on treasure and used them to study geography, science, and English.
We wrote about treasure and learned about pirates. It was a blast!

---

[11] Jim Elliot, "He is no fool who gives…" *Goodreads*. Date of access: September
5, 2023 (https://www.goodreads.com/quotes/2919-he-is-no-fool-who-gives-what-
he-cannot-keep).

Each week I recorded a television show that was airing at the time called, *The Hunt for Amazing Treasures.* Each hour-long episode contained four fifteen-minute segments on people who had discovered something of great value, and one in particular contained a segment about some fishermen from Mississippi who had discovered a sunken treasure accidentally. One day they were reeling in their huge commercial fishing net when they realized that it was ripped. Clumps of debris had gotten caught in it and fell to the deck of their ship.

However, upon closer examination, these clumps of debris turned out to be clumps of silver coins. They then discovered that the coins came from a wreck below, the *El Cazador*, a Spanish galleon that had been enroute from Veracuz, Mexico to New Orleans in 1783.

The *El Cazador* had a cargo hold full of silver coins intended to pay the salaries of soldiers who would assist in fueling the Spanish war efforts against the French, under Napoleon's command. Some historians believe that had the *El Cazador* made it to New Orleans with its precious cargo, Spain might not have given the territory back to France in 1801. And, in turn, the United States would not have been able to acquire it for $15 million in 1803 from the French in the Louisiana Purchase. This incident has since been called, *The Shipwreck That Changed the History of the World*.

In the documentary, the camera panned across a large vault filled with silver coins that the fishermen had retrieved from the wreck. There were thousands of them! I thought that perhaps if so many coins had been found, they could be available for purchase. Upon searching online, I discovered that in fact some of the coins *were* for sale. The prices varied depending on their size and condition.

I sent a quick email to the owners, explaining who I was. I proposed a partnership of sorts. My students would collect "treasure" from their neighborhood, in the form of recyclable cans and bottles, and redeem them for paper replicas of the coins from the *El Cazador*. Each paper replica would hold the name of the student who had earned it, after which it would be placed in a treasure chest in the classroom. At the end of the contest, these replicas would be drawn from the chest and students would have the opportunity to win real sunken treasure from the *El Cazador*, which we would purchase using the money we'd made from the recycled cans and bottles.

A few days later, I received a reply. The family-owned fishing company who now owned the rights to the *El Cazador* treasure said that they had met to discuss my proposal. They liked my idea so much that they were willing to sell me coins at an incredibly low price!

Overjoyed, I proceeded to run this contest with my students. I continued doing this for several years, until I finally retired from teaching.

Allow me to share one more treasure story. One weekend when my kids were young, I went with them to some neighborhood garage sales. They loved garage sales because they always came home with some new toy or piece of sports equipment.

Just around the corner from our home, an entire street had organized a collective sale. I was immediately drawn to one house in particular, where I noticed a large table full of sports cards. Really full! I had collected sports cards off and on since I was a kid and always thought of my collection as being a sort of backup retirement plan for when I got old. Hopefully by then the cards would have appreciated so much in value that I could sell them and live comfortably on the proceeds. Hey, dreams are free!

I looked with interest through the cards and asked the young seller, who was still in the process of arranging them, how many cards he had. He replied that he had almost thirteen thousand NHL hockey cards, all in mint condition and from the early 1990's.

"How much do you want for them?" I asked.

I was surprised by his answer: "Make me an offer."

I had no idea what such a sizeable collection was worth, so I threw out a number, fully expecting to be laughed at. This was a price I didn't expect him to accept.

During the negotiations, I had noticed the boy's parents standing a few feet behind him, watching our interaction with interest.

To my surprise, he increased the price only slightly from my offer. He then threw in five oak boxes that his dad had made to store the cards.

"Deal!" I blurted out as I reached out to shake his hand.

I had to return home to get the money, agreeing to be back in a few minutes. In the meantime, he would start packing up the cards.

I fully expected to return and have the entire deal collapse, but to my delight most of the cards had been packed into boxes upon my return. The table was emptying quickly.

As I helped him box up the remaining cards, I asked why he was selling such a large collection. He replied that he was soon heading off to university and simply no longer had any interest in them. They were taking up valuable space and he wanted the money instead.

We loaded the last boxes into my car and I immediately drove to a nearby convenience store, where I purchased a magazine that listed the current values of specific sports cards. I wanted to estimate the value of the collection.

When I arrived home, I pulled out hundreds of rookie cards from some of the best players in the NHL. These cards alone were worth several hundred dollars. I estimated the value of the whole collection, at that time, to be in the thousands. I was ecstatic, to say the least!

As I reflect on that experience, two things stand out in my mind. I remember the feeling I had as I drove away from this garage sale with a trunkful of several thousand mint-condition hockey cards. I felt as though I had just found an amazing treasure. The euphoria and adrenaline rush was unbelievable!

I also remember how fleeting that feeling was. Everything went back to normal quickly. Those cards are still sitting in boxes in my basement, collecting dust. Hopefully they are rising in value as they get older—but they probably aren't. Maybe someday I'll cash them in for actual money or sell them to someone who wants them more than I do.

I've had this feeling before. Usually it's after purchasing something I've had my eye on for quite some time. All the dreaming and planning that went into making the Big Purchase often ends in buyer's remorse. The excitement fades when the item doesn't quite meet expectations. It doesn't make me feel as good as I thought it would.

Disappointment. Hollow dreams. Wasted money.

Is it any wonder Jesus talked about treasure the way He did? He knows just how much of a "god" money and possessions can be to us. He knows how difficult it is for us to serve God and place Him first in our lives when our money and possessions so easily take first place among our priorities. In fact, fifteen percent of everything Jesus talked about in the Bible was related to money and possessions!

Basically, the gist of what He said regarding this topic could be summarized in just a few verses. He tells a story about a traveler who stumbles upon an amazing treasure while on a journey:

> The kingdom of heaven is like treasure hidden in a field. When a man found it, he hid it again, and then in his joy went and sold all he had and bought that field. (Matthew 13:44)

This traveler knew how important his newfound treasure was. He knew that it was worthy of him risking everything he owned in order to possess it. Nothing was more important to him than pursuing the Kingdom of Heaven—his relationship with his Creator!

In another example, a rich man once asked Jesus how to inherit eternal life. Jesus responded, *"If you want to be perfect, go, sell your possessions and give to the poor, and you will have treasure in heaven. Then come, follow me"* (Matthew 19:21). He knew how important money and possessions were to the man—and that the man wouldn't be able to serve God unless he dethroned his money idol. Giving his money to the poor was not the point. Rather, he wasn't going to be able to earn his salvation that way.

Sadly, the man walked away feeling dejected because he was unwilling to place God above his money and possessions. He had priority issues!

Lastly, Jesus reminds us where our treasure should be stored:

Do not store up for yourselves treasures on earth, where moths and vermin destroy, and where thieves break in and steal. But store up for yourselves treasures in heaven, where moths and vermin do not destroy, and where thieves do not break in and steal. For where your treasure is, there your heart will be also. (Matthew 6:19–21)

So what is this treasure we need to store in heaven? If the pursuit of money and earthly possessions aren't important in the big scheme of things, what *is* important?

When Jesus talked about the kind of treasure we should store in heaven, He was referring to things that will last for eternity. He knew that everything on earth is temporary and will ultimately fade into dust. We can't take our possessions with us when we die.

The only thing that will last for eternity is our relationship with Him! The closer our relationship to Him, the more our treasure grows in heaven. God wants us to know and love Him, and to love others as well. It's that simple!

Jesus made this clear when He was asked what the greatest commandment is. He replied, *"'Love the Lord your God with all your heart and with all your soul and with all your mind.' This is the first and greatest commandment"* (Matthew 22:37–38). He followed this by saying: *"And the second is like it: 'Love your neighbor as yourself'"* (Matthew 22:39).

I had to honestly ask myself where Jesus sat on my priority list. Were there "treasures" in my life—money, possessions, family, friends, entertainment, work, etc. — that took priority over my relationship with Him? If so, how could I rearrange my list to place my priorities in the correct order?

I discovered that this process begins in the heart. After realizing what's really important in the Big Picture, it was time for me to put my priorities in order. Without taking action to develop my relationship with Jesus, nothing would change. I needed to make conscious choices to implement a plan, focus on growing my treasures in heaven, and begin moving towards building a close relationship with Him.

This has now become my number one priority.

Is it yours? Where does your relationship with our Creator rank on your list of priorities? Where on your list are money and possessions? What is your top priority? These are important questions to ask yourself if you're serious about learning and applying *The Most Important Lesson*.

NINE
IT'S ALL ABOUT PRIORITIES

To change your life, you need to
change your priorities.[12]
—Mark Twain

So I've got a new goal in life. I have an updated list of priorities and have been given a second chance. I don't want to waste it! After all, that would be more foolish than missing the goal the first time.

It always amazes me to see people do things, or avoid doing things, that they know could benefit them. Why do people continue with self-destructive behaviors when they know better? By making a change, often a very minor change, they could improve the quality of their lives. For some reason, they make the choice not to.

Considering the resources we have available to us today, we have no excuse to go through life uneducated. We can't blame ignorance for our problems.

Knowing this, my first course of action towards getting to know Jesus better was to talk to friends, many of them church pastors, and get their recommendations for books I should read. The list became very long, very quickly.

---

[12] Mark Twain, "101 Quotes to Get Your Priorities Right," *Calendar.com*. June 3, 2021 (https://www.calendar.com/blog/101-quotes-to-get-your-priorities-right).

You should know right off the bat that I am not an avid reader. If I can learn something by watching a video on YouTube, I'll choose that every time. The concept of reading a huge list of books was not attractive to me.

I recently read that the average book contains sixty-four thousand words. The average person reads about two hundred to two hundred fifty words per minute. Therefore, it should take about three hundred twenty minutes to read a book cover to cover. If you break that down and divide it by seven (the number of days in a week), that's approximately forty-five minutes per day to read a book in one week.

That little bit of mathematical motivation helped me create a new target. If I read at least twenty to thirty minutes per day, I could complete one book every two weeks. In a year, I could get through twenty-six books, each one geared to help me learn how to get closer to Jesus. That may seem like a lot to some of you, and it's also not nearly enough to many others. But for me, that's approximately twenty-six more books per year than I was reading before!

Along the way, I've also discovered tons of valuable resources on YouTube covering any topic you can imagine, including how to get close to Jesus. The problem with YouTube, though—and the internet in general—is that you need to be careful about filtering the good from the bad. And there is a lot of really bad stuff out there!

I looked for, and found, some reliable Christian sources online that serve as a constant source of encouragement and education. To better protect myself, and assist with the vetting process, I often compare what these sources teach to the Bible, to ensure that their teaching measures up to the truth of God's Word.

My biggest revelation, however, may come as a no-brainer. One day I asked myself, "How do you get to know someone better?" The first thing that popped into my head was easy: "Simply learn more about them."

So how do you learn about Jesus? Well, why not start by going straight to the source—the New Testament? After all, this text contains the story of Jesus. It contains the lessons He taught and the testimonials of those who interacted with Him. It contains the words He actually spoke! Everything else is simply a commentary, supplemental to what has already been written in Scripture.

The Bible is full of references to the cultural nuances that make a big difference in understanding Jesus's lessons. He was a master at making these lessons relevant to the people with whom He communicated, many of whom weren't highly educated. They needed to hear these lessons in simple, relatable terms. Jesus knew this.

For us in the twenty-first century, a few history lessons can assist us in better understanding the lessons Jesus taught.

I have always struggled to find time to do devotions. In fact, I hate that phrase—"do devotions." It takes something meaningful and turns it into a task to check off my to-do list each day. Is this how I treat my other relationships?

Too often I've reduced my quiet time with God to a five-minute ritual in order to ease my conscience. After all, this is what all good Christians do, right? How would your kids or spouse feel if you squeezed in a five-minute conversation with them each day because you felt like you *had* to? How well would your relationships develop with them? Would you even have those relationships at all?

So why do we do this to God—our Creator, Protector, and Savior?

If getting to know Jesus is the most important lesson I will ever learn, then why isn't it my first priority in life?

Following my death experience, I had to ask myself why I didn't make time on a daily basis to do something so important. Why wouldn't I make spending time with Jesus as big a priority as breathing and eating? Why would I let so many trivial things in life get in the way of my pursuit of Him?

It was time to shake things up and get my priorities in order. I needed to take an accounting of my life so I could place the most important priorities right at the top. These needed to be non-negotiables. If I truly believed this to be the most important thing, it should come first.

I now start each day by spending time with Jesus, right after making a cup of freshly brewed coffee! This coffee time with Jesus—reading His Word, learning about Him, and talking to Him through prayer—has become a daily routine, something I look forward to with anticipation!

I've learned something important from the apostle Paul about reading the Bible. When reading, I must ask the Holy Spirit to open my eyes so I might see the truth of His Word, open my ears so I might hear His voice speaking to me, open my mind so I might understand what I'm reading, and open my heart so I might be receptive to His transforming power in my life.

Not to sound too cliché, but my days usually go better when I start them with Jesus!

Another big change I've made is to talk to Jesus as much as possible throughout the day. Prayer, or the simple act of talking to Jesus, isn't just something we should do for a few minutes before drifting off to sleep at night. It's not about repeating a memorized ditty before each meal. Prayer is about having an actual conversation with God, our Creator.

Again, liken it to a human relationship with someone you love. You talk to them throughout the day. You talk to them about important stuff. You talk to them about problems you may be having and celebrate with them when things go great. Some conversations are longer than others. Sometimes you talk. Sometimes you listen.

Well, it should be no different with Jesus.

The apostle Paul reminds us in 1 Thessalonians 5:17 that we are to pray continuously—not just before meals, just before bed, when we need something, or when we're in trouble. It must be *continuous*. Practicing continuous prayer has allowed me to take a huge step in the right direction with Jesus. In fact, I often find myself praying without even realizing it! As someone comes to mind, I often just talk to Jesus about them. When I wake up in the middle of the night, I'll go to prayer and talk about whatever has been keeping me awake, or whatever pops into my mind. Sometimes I'll simply say, "What do You want to say to me, Lord?" Prayer has an amazing way of calming and soothing the racing mind.

Prayer is powerful! James 5:16 declares, *"The prayer of a righteous man is powerful and effective."* The Bible is full of accounts that describe the power of prayer. The power of prayer has overcome enemies (Psalm 6:9–10), conquered death (2 Kings 4:3–36), brought healing (James 5:14–15), and defeated demons (Mark 9:29). God, through prayer, opens eyes, changes hearts, heals wounds, and grants wisdom (James 1:5). The power of prayer should never be underestimated, because it draws on the glory and might of the infinitely powerful God of the universe!

Many books on the topic of prayer have been written by far wiser people than myself. I'd encourage you to read some of them to help you fully understand the benefits of a vibrant prayer life. It will help you to become closer to Jesus.

Since beginning this new relationship with Jesus, the Bible has come alive to me. I understand things now that I never understood before. Passages I'd read many times in the past have taken on a whole new meaning. I comprehend and retain what I read better than ever before. I truly thirst for my time in the Word and enjoy it.

The Bible isn't just a book. It's a living text that comes straight from God. It's like food to a starving person.

Bon appetit!

TEN

FORGIVING AND FORGETTING
IS FOUNDATIONAL

To forgive is to set a prisoner free and discover
that the prisoner was you.[13]
—Lewis B. Smedes

I love taking personality tests, mainly because I'm curious to see how accurate they are. It often becomes more of a competition than an exercise in self-realization. Can answering a few questions accurately define my personality and describe who I really am? We'll see!

Not long ago, I did one that analyzed my personality based on which colors I liked and disliked. I was surprised at how accurate it was. Who knew that you could learn things about people by their favorite colors? Sometimes I get the feeling that certain tests only *appear* to be accurate by offering ambiguous results, similar to how psychics read people's palms. Yes, someone close to me is ill. And yes, I am planning on taking a trip in the not-too-distant future...

Most of the tests I've taken, however, are pretty accurate at describing me and how I think. A few years ago, I took a personality test by Gallup called StrengthsFinder. The test was designed to help

---

[13] Lewis B. Smedes, "To Forgive Is to Set a Prisoner Free," *Successful Spirit*. December 23, 2022 (https://www.thesuccessfulspirit.com/to-forgive-is-to-set-a-prisoner-free).

me become more engaged at work, more productive in my roles, happier, and healthier.[14] It's a great test to help you better understand how you think and react in certain situations.

Through this test, I learned that my number one strength is competition. This was no surprise to me—or anyone who knows me well, for that matter!

I tell you this to help you better understand the lens through which I view life in general. Competition, and the desire to win, has been part of my DNA from my earliest memories. It's a good strength to have if you're into sports, flying fighter jets, or wrestling alligators for a living.

But one of the problems with possessing a strength like this is that everything in life becomes a competition where you view yourself as either winning or losing. People, even loved ones, can be viewed as competitors even though there's nothing to compete over.

Unfortunately, I have found myself unintentionally hurting people or damaging relationships over the years through my desire to always come out on top. And this eventually led me to develop issues with self-forgiveness.

We most commonly think of forgiveness as an action that involves other people. Maybe someone harmed or offended you in some way, putting you in the position of having to choose whether to forgive them. This is not an easy task. Our first reaction is often bent towards revenge and retribution.

The Bible is pretty clear on forgiveness. The foundation of our belief system as Christians is based on the fact that Jesus Christ died for the forgiveness of our sins. God forgives freely and expects His children to do likewise. We should not feel condemnation of any kind. If we belong to Christ, we are free. Romans 8:1 states, *"Therefore, there is now no condemnation for those who are in Christ Jesus."*

---

[14] "Strengths Finder," *Gallup*. Date of access: September 5, 2023 (https://www.gallup.com/cliftonstrengths/en/strengthsfinder.aspx).

Christ will convict you of sin but will not condemn you once you've asked for His forgiveness. You're not condemned. However, you do need Jesus, because *"through Christ Jesus the law of the Spirit who gives life has set you free from the law of sin and death"* (Romans 8:2).

Unfortunately, strong feelings of self-condemnation can manifest when we struggle to forgive ourselves. Feelings often arise that tell us, "I'm not good enough. I should have done better. I should have known better." Please know that these thoughts don't come from God. They come from a place of pain, hurt, or fear that often stays buried deep inside. They go against God's nature, making us feel guilty or ashamed of our past mistakes.

The sacrifice of His Son, Jesus, was made so the entire world could be forgiven and restored in relationship back to Him. We deserve punishment because of our sins, but Jesus paid our debt and took the punishment for us.

The enemy, satan, loves nothing more than to attack our minds with feelings of inadequacy, guilt, and condemnation. Our minds are a battleground. This is why the apostle Paul encourages us to think about good things:

Finally, brothers and sisters, whatever is true, whatever is noble, whatever is right, whatever is pure, whatever is lovely, whatever is admirable—if anything is excellent or praiseworthy—think about such things. (Philippians 4:8)

How we perceive things starts in the mind, so we must guard our thoughts.

When God forgives us, the Bible says that He forgets our sins. Period. He chooses not to hold our sins against us or bring them up in a negative way in the future. So if He makes this promise, why do we so often have difficulty forgiving ourselves?

This is an issue I have struggled with most of my life! It has prevented me from moving forward the way God designed.

The first step in the process of forgiving ourselves is realizing that God wants us to become all that He created us to be. We cannot change the past and we may not be able to undo what we've done, but we can begin the process of change by making better choices. Since God has blessed us with a free will, we need to make the choice to forgive in order to heal. Healing is important to God, and it begins with forgiveness. When we start by accepting Christ's forgiveness, we can introduce real change into our lives by forgiving ourselves.

One of my favorite verses is Matthew 22:39, which instructs us to love our neighbors as ourselves. With this passage, Jesus meant to help us gain a better perspective on treating others with the same love, mercy, and forgiveness we extend to ourselves. The problem is that if we harbor negative feelings and emotions toward ourselves, we will likely do the same toward others.

We are required to forgive others. This is not an option. This is a command from God.

> For if you forgive other people when they sin against you, your heavenly Father will also forgive you. But if you do not forgive others their sins, your Father will not forgive your sins. (Matthew 6:14–15)

God doesn't tell us to forgive others because He wants to make our lives miserable. He does so because He wants us to experience freedom—His freedom.

A wise person once said that not forgiving someone is like drinking poison and expecting the other person to die. Only a fool would do this! Harboring unforgiveness hurts us more than it hurts anyone else.

One of the best books I've ever read on the topic of forgiveness is R.T. Kendall's *Total Forgiveness*. He writes,

When Jesus said, "If you forgive men when they sin against you, your Heavenly Father will also forgive you," He was not talking about how to achieve salvation. He was referring to receiving the anointing of God and participating in an intimate relationship with the Father. Unless we are walking in a state of forgiveness toward others, we cannot be in an intimate relationship with God.[15]

So what exactly is forgiveness? It's a choice to release an offender from punishment and entrust the matter to God. As Christians, we have been forgiven for our offences through Christ taking the punishment for our sin by dying on the cross. Christ paid our fine in the courts of heaven. His work on the cross cancels our debt.

Forgiveness is also unconditional. We need to forgive regardless of whether the offender apologizes or takes responsibility. In other words, our ability to forgive is not dependent on the actions of others. It is a choice *we* make!

There are many benefits to forgiveness, far too many for me to get into in this chapter. Suffice it to say that the person who gains the most from forgiveness is the person who does the forgiving. God also commands us to forgive, and He only makes commandments for His people's sake. He wants the best for us! The benefits of forgiveness include blessings, freedom, and better relationships. Forgiveness improves our physical and mental health. It also starts us on the road to healing and allows us to live in the present.

It is no accident that when Jesus taught us how to pray on a daily basis, through the Lord's Prayer, he said, *"Forgive us our sins, for we also forgive everyone who sins against us"* (Luke 11:4).

In order to develop intimacy with Jesus, forgiveness needs to be a priority in your life. If you have an issue of unforgiveness, I urge you

---

[15] R.T. Kendall, *Total Forgiveness* (Lake Mary, FL: Charisma House, 2007), 87.

to do whatever is necessary to deal with it. The sooner you deal with it, the healthier and happier you will be!

Ask for God's help and He'll show you how.

ELEVEN

PAY ATTENTION TO RED FLAGS

Recognize warning signs or prepare
to be blindsided.[16]
—Frank Sonnenberg

Joanne and I got our first professional jobs as teachers in 1987 at a school for ex-patriots in Tripoli, Libya. It wasn't an easy time to live in Libya. The year prior to our arrival, the United States had conducted bombing missions in Tripoli in retaliation for Libya's leader, Muammar Ghadafi, sending his country's jets into an international no-fly zone. Consequently, all American teachers vacated Libya, creating openings for us to fill. Worldwide economic sanctions were levied against Libya and their international trade ceased. This limited the quantity and quality of food and other products made available in the country. It was a difficult place to live.

There was, however, an expat scuba diving club in Tripoli that met on a weekly basis as a social outlet. The club even had some instructor-level dive masters from other countries. They conducted lessons to help members advance their skills. Each weekend we gathered as a group and went diving in the Mediterranean.

---

[16] Frank Sonnenberg, "Recognize warning signs..." *Facebook*. January 12, 2022 (https://www.facebook.com/FrankSonnenbergOnline/posts/349983500461981).

This was certainly one of the highlights of my time in Libya. I looked forward to the meetings, and especially the weekend dives. The dive locations changed each week and we were able to explore different stretches of the Mediterranean coast. Some sites were near ancient Roman ruins, which made the adventures even more enjoyable! Indeed, the Libyan coast is home to some of the best-preserved Roman ruins in the world.

One particular weekend, we gathered to follow each other out to a new dive location. I was disappointed that none of the leaders were able to join us that day, but there was safety in numbers since several other club members showed up. We drove approximately an hour to the site, unloaded all our equipment, and prepared for the dive. As usual, it was going to be a shore dive, meaning that we would enter the water from the shore and walk out with our dive buddy far enough to get into deep water and then submerge.

The weather that day was sunny but windy. The temperature rose steadily as it was getting close to noon by the time we arrived. It wasn't uncommon for temperatures to reach well past 40°C (104°F).

Joanne decided not to dive that day and instead hung out on the beach while I buddied up with another diver. After getting into our suits and checking each other's equipment, we trekked into the water. The rest of the divers in the club did likewise.

The first thing I noticed were the whitecaps on the water. This was not a good sign. Whitecaps can make the entry and exit precarious, but I felt that we had driven too far to be turned back by mildly rough seas.

As soon as I get underwater, the whitecaps will become a non-issue, I thought.

As we trudged into the sea, I was surprised to see how shallow the water was… and how far we had to trek in order to find water deep enough for us to submerge. Carrying a tank on my back and wearing a weight belt with thirty extra pounds around my waist made the walk difficult, especially under the hot midday sun. I struggled to stay upright as the wind and waves wreaked havoc on my top-heavy body.

 The next red flag were the globs of heavy crude oil we encountered the further out we waded. It was obvious there had been an oil spill from one of the many freighters offshore. Libya was one of the world's leading oil producers, and these large freighters were a common sight. The globs were approximately two to four centimeters in length and stuck to us like glue. My dive buddy and I surmised that they were floating atop the water and would no longer be an issue under the surface.

 By the time we reached water deep enough for us to begin our dive, we had trudged about three hundred fifty meters from shore. I paused to put my dive mask on and noticed that the front glass was covered with oil. I took it off and tried to clean it, but the effort was futile. The saltwater wasn't sufficient to clean the sticky oil, and rubbing the mask only made it worse.

 I told my dive buddy that I wouldn't be able to continue with the dive because I couldn't see out of my mask. I would need to head back to shore immediately. He acknowledged my request but insisted on continuing his dive without me. As I turned and started my long solo trek back to shore, he donned his mask and disappeared underwater.

 By now I was getting pretty tired. The heat, combined with the burden of the weight belt, tank, and other equipment, was taking a toll on me. The wind caused the waves to push me to and fro and I struggled to stay upright. Realizing that this was a waste of energy, I inflated my buoyancy compensator, turned over onto my back, and started kicking with my fins. Periodically I turned to reference the shore and gauge my progress.

 For some reason, I wasn't getting any closer to shore.

 Seconds turned into minutes, and with each kick my energy level decreased. The wind and waves were picking up, and seawater mixed with crude oil splashed onto my face, coating my nose, eyes, and mouth. I began to swallow water, fighting to keep my head above the surface. I tried to put my regulator in my mouth so I could keep breathing, but the regulator was clogged with oil.

I turned again to check how close I was to shore. No progress.

That's when I surmised that I was caught in an undertow current. Despite my efforts over the past fifteen minutes, the currents were actually taking me further out. Things were getting dire!

On the verge of panic, and realizing that my situation was life-threatening, I knew that panicking would be the end of me. I tried my best to stay calm and think through my options.

I struggled to catch my breath just before my head went under again, possibly for the last time.

Suddenly I heard a small voice inside my head: *"Drop your weight belt."*

I quickly reached down and flipped the buckle that secured my weight belt. It fell off immediately. The release of the additional thirty pounds instantly caused me to become more buoyant.

I now had hope.

Thrusting my head above the water, I sucked in a deep breath of air. I kicked with all I had for the next few minutes. When I turned to measure my progress, the shore looked a bit closer! This served as a source of encouragement. I reached down deep to tap into the last bit of adrenaline I could muster, then continued kicking with everything I had.

After another minute, I looked again and realized that I just might make it!

Covered in crude oil, I eventually reached water shallow enough that I could kneel for a while to regain my strength.

Eventually I made it to shore, completely and totally exhausted. I lay on the sand for quite some time before I was able to stand again and walk down the beach to where Joanne was waiting. She had no idea what had happened.

When I finally reached her, she had a worried look on her face and could tell I'd been through a rough experience. We sat together on the beach as I told her what I'd just gone through.

Partway into my story, we were alerted to a situation at the water's edge directly in front of us. Several dive club members were assisting a middle-aged woman get out of the water. We rushed over to see if we could help only to discover that crude oil had gotten into her regulator. Her air supply had cut off when she was approximately seventy-five feet down. Fortunately, she survived the incident, but things could easily have turned out disastrously if not for the quick thinking of her fellow divers. Praise God!

We all learned some valuable lessons that day. As a group of novice divers, we had allowed ourselves to get overconfident, thinking we had safety in numbers. Despite being adults, we'd felt a measure of peer pressure to proceed with the dive despite the warning signs.

In retrospect, any number of red flags should have prevented us from carrying on with the dive. The lack of an experienced dive instructor. The unfamiliar site. The high winds and whitecaps on the water. The crude oil. In my case, getting separated from my dive buddy. None of these warning signs stopped us from barreling headfirst into a dangerous situation. It almost cost the lives of two club members.

As I reflect on this incident many years later, I have 20/20 vision. I ask myself how I could have been so naïve. How could I not have seen the dangers right in front of me? Why did I press on when I recognized so many risks? Why hadn't I been willing to sacrifice my useless air tank and buoyancy compensator for the sake of saving my own life? How much easier would it have been to move forward if I had dropped them and proceeded with just my fins!

But hindsight is always 20/20.

I have no doubt that it was God who whispered to me the life-saving advice to drop my weight belt. He had been watching the whole thing unfold step by step.

How often do we ignore warning signs that impede the progress of our relationship with Jesus? Satan wants nothing more than to mess up our lives, especially our relationship with Jesus. We have a real enemy whose aim is to steal, kill, and destroy (John 10:10). He whispers lies to us and looks for opportunities to deceive us any chance he gets (John 8:44).

The Bible makes it clear that satan makes war against us when we keep God's commands and set our eyes on Jesus.

The Bible also instructs us in how to defeat the enemy. According to Revelation 12:11, we defeat satan through worshiping with our mouths and having a close relationship with Jesus. By following Jesus and doing what He says, no attack from satan is ever strong enough to knock us down.

> For I am convinced that neither death nor life, neither angels nor demons, neither the present nor the future, nor any powers, neither height nor depth, nor anything else in all creation, will be able to separate us from the love of God that is in Christ Jesus our Lord. (Romans 8:38–39)

If you see any red flags along your journey towards a closer relationship with Jesus, know that He may have put them there to prevent you from experiencing something highly destructive. Don't ignore them! They are there for a reason. Deal with them as they arise or you may end up with some problems you never saw coming.

The next chapter may help you deal with these red flags when they arise.

TWELVE
HOW DO WE GET ATTACKED?

The enemy wouldn't be attacking you if something
very valuable wasn't inside of you. Thieves don't
break into empty houses.[17]
—Rick Godwin

Following the attack on Pearl Harbor in December 1941, Japan desired a single battle that would completely eradicate the Allies' ability to fight. Admiral Isoroku Yamamoto had no intention of fighting a prolonged war. He intended for the Pacific War to last no more than one hundred fifty days, fearing that the longer the war went on, the lower the chance of a Japanese victory.

His intention was to attack Midway Atoll, in the middle of the northern Pacific Ocean, with a deceptively large force that would surprise and destroy the United States' fleet. With this battle behind them, the Japanese would have easy access to attacking the U.S. mainland.

However, the U.S. Navy was prepared for the attack.

---

[17] Rick Godwin, "The enemy wouldn't be attacking…" *Everyday Simple Truths*. Date of access: September 5, 2023 (https://everydaysimpletruths.com/2017/02/20/the-enemy-wouldnt-be-attacking-you-if-something-very-valuable-wasnt-inside-of-you-thieves-dont-break-into-empty-houses-by-rick-godwin).

With the help of codebreakers and intelligence officers, the commander-in-chief of the U.S. Pacific Fleet, Admiral Chester Nimitz, was able to accurately deduce the size of the Japanese fleet, as well as their intentions. As a result, the Allies were able to inflict devastating losses on Japan, who had committed four aircraft carriers, with 248 aircraft on them. They lost all of them.

The battle at Midway forced the Japanese to assume a defensive posture for the remainder of the war. Their battles inched incrementally closer to Japan, lacking the resources to stage a large-scale counteroffensive.

British historian, John Keegan, stated, "Within exactly five minutes... the whole course of the war in the Pacific had been reversed."[18]

When heading into battle, it's always a good idea to know how the enemy operates. If you understand their strategies and tactics you'll be better prepared to face them head-on.

Knowing this, we should be aware of the various ways in which satan works. He attacks believers when he thinks it will be to his advantage. This includes the period of time immediately following a great spiritual experience (Matthew 3:16, 17; 4:1), or right before someone is about to begin a new spiritual venture (Matthew 4:17). He also attacks when believers are vulnerable either physically or mentally (Matthew 4:2–3), or when they're alone (Matthew 4:1). We must always be on guard.

Satan's main form of attack is to get us to destroy ourselves from within. By planting seeds in our thoughts, he can grow them into destructive weeds, with us providing the fertilizer! Here's how he does it.

- Dangerous thoughts enter our minds, and we usually have no control over them. These seeds take root when the enemy makes the thoughts personal.

---

[18] John Keegan, "Carrier Battle: Midway," *Erenow.net*. Date of access: September 5, 2023 (https://erenow.net/ww/thesecondworldwarkeeganjohn/14.php).

- Once we dwell on a sinful thought, instead of rejecting it immediately we let it take root. We buy into satan's ideas and believe they're our own (Romans 7:15).
- The longer we dwell on it, the deeper the root grows. We consider how it would feel to act on the idea. We decide that we "have the right" to take the step. We justify our beliefs, saying, "Everyone has faults and secret sin." We get comfortable with the idea. We may even start to question whether God's Word is true.
- We act on what was previously only a thought, allowing the destructive process to begin. Satan disguises the full extent of our sin and the spiritual erosion it causes. We're often deceived about the devastation our sin causes.
- We justify the action, behavior, or thinking. We're swallowed up by sin and don't intend to change, no matter how painful the consequences.
- Over time we're consumed by guilt, resentment, bitterness, and anxiety. Sin's destructiveness takes its toll.

Do you need a better reason to get close to Jesus? If you knew that someone was bent on harming you to the point of death, would it not be prudent to do everything in your power to protect yourself?

Submit yourselves, then, to God. Resist the devil, and he will flee from you. (James 4:7)

Getting close to Jesus is the best way to protect ourselves from satan's attacks. God makes it clear that He has prepared us for this spiritual battle. As our Commander-in-Chief, He would never send His soldiers into battle unprepared or ill-equipped.

He has given us a battle plan through His Word and protective armor to wear proudly.

Finally, be strong in the Lord and in his mighty power. Put on the full armor of God, so that you can take your stand against the devil's schemes. For our struggle is not against flesh and blood, but against the rulers, against the authorities, against the powers of this dark world and against the spiritual forces of evil in the heavenly realms. Therefore put on the full armor of God, so that when the day of evil comes, you may be able to stand your ground, and after you have done everything, to stand. Stand firm then, with the belt of truth buckled around your waist, with the breastplate of righteousness in place, and with your feet fitted with the readiness that comes from the gospel of peace. In addition to all this, take up the shield of faith, with which you can extinguish all the flaming arrows of the evil one. Take the helmet of salvation and the sword of the Spirit, which is the word of God. (Ephesians 6:10–17)

God asks each one of us to put on the whole armor He has provided. Through this metaphor, we perceive a soldier putting on armor in preparation for battle. Similarly, the Apostle Paul points to the fact that every person on this earth is under spiritual attack from the evil one.

Therefore, we are encouraged to wear the armor of God. We need to put it on every day before we do anything, whether at home, school, work, or any other context. Just like the armor protects the soldier, this armor protects all who believe in Jesus from the spiritual forces of darkness.

God has won the war, but we still fight battles along the way. The closer you get to Jesus, the better prepared you'll be to enter the battle.

THIRTEEN
THE SECOND DREAM

I had a dream that made me afraid. As I was
lying in bed, the images and visions that passed
through my mind terrified me.
—Daniel 4:5

Approximately three months after my heart attack, I had a second dream. Just like the first one, it had to do with hockey.

I was on my way to a big, professional arena to play hockey. Upon entering the dressing room, I once again realized that I didn't have my stick. Following the familiar self-condemnation routine about being unprepared and forgetting such an essential piece of equipment, I calculated how long it would take to drive home, get my stick, and return to the arena. If I left right away and drove quickly, I could get back by the end of the first period.

I ran up a long staircase to the exit. Once I got to the parking lot, all I could see were broken hockey sticks, one beside every vehicle. There were hundreds of them! When I got to my car, much to my surprise, I discovered two hockey sticks lying on the ground beside the driver's door. They were in perfect condition. I wouldn't have to drive home after all!

I grabbed the sticks and ran back to the arena. Already I could see my teammates warming up on the ice. I put on my equipment as quickly as I could and entered the game just as it started.

I had the best game of my life! I was able to score at will, but as the game neared its end I was surprised to see that all the other players on the ice were young children. No wonder I could outplay them so easily!

It took me a long time to process this dream. Over a year in fact. I had no idea what it meant, if anything. I'm not one to try and interpret dreams just for the sake of satisfying my curiosity.

But this dream was different. After talking with many close friends and pastors, I felt that this one required some effort to discern the meaning.

I decided there was no better source of clarification than God Himself. After all, He has used dreams to communicate to His people for centuries. Why could He not do the same for me?

In fact, there are twenty-one dreams recorded in the Bible. God not only provided dreams in order to direct people, He also gave some the ability to interpret dreams.

A good example of this is found in the story of Joseph (Genesis 37–50), one of my favorite stories in the Bible, which demonstrates how God used six different dreams to accomplish His purpose through Joseph.

Joseph was sold into slavery by his jealous brothers and rose to become the second most powerful man in Egypt next to Pharaoh. Joseph's presence and powerful position saved his entire family by causing his father, Jacob, to eventually leave Canaan and settle in Egypt.

A few days after praying for God to reveal to me the significance and meaning of this second dream, I was again awakened in the middle of the night. It seems that 4:00 a.m. is the time when God likes to talk to me! This is when I tend to hear from Him most clearly.

Here is what I was shown. As in previous dreams, the hockey sticks I forgot to bring represented my state of unpreparedness for death (or Christ's return). The broken sticks in the parking lot represented wasted time, squandered opportunities to grow closer to Jesus. They also represented the wasted opportunities of those around me, those who have heard the message of salvation, ignored it, or even rejected it.

The hockey sticks I found lying beside my car represented my newfound hope and revelation. They represented the fact that I had discovered what I needed to do to best prepare for eternity. I now know the importance of developing a close relationship with Jesus. I know the urgency of developing that relationship as quickly as possible.

And finally, the success I experienced in the game, served as confirmation that I had found the secret to what is really important in life. God has given me the ability to thrive through knowing Him intimately. I had finally learned the most important lesson of my life!

Once more, God had spoken to me through a dream and confirmed that I was on the right track. Just as Jesus used parables to communicate to people in His day, in language they could understand, God spoke to me through a dream I could relate to.

FOURTEEN
SO WHERE DO YOU START?

Therefore, if anyone is in Christ, he is a new
creation; old things have passed away;
behold, all things have become new.
—2 Corinthians 5:17

If you've made it this far in the book, awesome! Something must have caught your attention. However, you may still have some questions about what it means to be a Christian—or more accurately, a follower of Christ.

Throughout the book, I've dropped hints about what it takes to ensure that your sins will be forgiven and you'll be in right standing with our Creator, guaranteeing you a place in heaven.

Let me take a few moments to share with you exactly what the gospel is, so there is no confusion. It is critical for everyone to understand the gospel clearly and fully comprehend the consequences of either accepting it or doing nothing and thereby rejecting it.

What is the gospel? The word literally means "good news" and occurs exclusively in the New Testament. The gospel, broadly speaking, is the whole of Scripture; more specifically, however, it's the good news concerning Christ and the way of salvation.

The key to understanding the gospel is to know why it's good news. To do that, we must first start with the bad news.

The Old Testament Law, including the Ten Commandments, was given to Israel during the time of Moses (Deuteronomy 5:1–22). The Law can be thought of as a measuring stick, and sin is anything that causes us to fall short of God's standard. The Law is so stringent that no human could possibly follow it perfectly, in letter or in spirit. Despite how good or bad we think we are, we are all in the same spiritual boat—we have sinned, and the punishment for sin is death, i.e. separation from God (Romans 3:23, 6:23). As a result, we are destined for an eternal punishment in hell, a place of unimaginable torment and suffering.

To go to heaven, our sin must be somehow removed or paid for. God's Law establishes that we can only be cleansed from sin through the bloody sacrifice of an innocent life (Hebrews 9:22).

Under the Law, animal sacrifices were offered year after year as a reminder of sin. They were a symbol of the coming sacrifice of Christ (Hebrews 10:3–4).

According to the gospel, Jesus died on the cross as a sin offering to fulfill the Law's righteous requirement (Romans 8:3–4, Hebrews 10:5–10). By offering Himself as a sacrifice for our sins, Jesus became a substitute for all who believe (Hebrews 10:11–18). The work of atonement for our sins is now finished, and that's good news. Our debt has been paid by Him.

The gospel also involves Jesus's resurrection on the third day. We read in Romans 4:25, *"He was delivered over to death for our sins and was raised to life for our justification."* The fact that Jesus conquered sin and death is great news, and the fact that He offers to share that victory with us is the greatest news of all (John 14:19).

To reject the gospel is to embrace the bad news. Condemnation by God is the result of failing to have faith in the Son of God, God's only provision for salvation.

For God did not send his Son into the world to condemn the world, but to save the world through him. Whoever believes in him is not condemned, but whoever does not believe stands condemned already because they have not believed in the name of God's one and only Son. (John 3:17–18)

God has given a doomed world good news: the gospel of Jesus Christ!

To sum everything up, it's tough to admit that we're wrong. Most of us feel that we are basically good and we like to think we are never as bad as some. The truth is that we are all sinners and can never be good enough to earn our way to heaven. God's Word clearly states that all have sinned. We've all done things that are wrong. We've all broken God's Law (Romans 3:23). Because God is holy and just, anyone who sins against Him deserves punishment. We are told in the Bible that the wages or payment for sin is death—eternal death in hell (Romans 6:23).

So what do we have to do to be saved? God made it so simple. There are three easy steps.

1. Admit that you are a sinner (Romans 3:23, Romans 6:23, Acts 3:19, 1 John 1:9). Both John the Baptist and Jesus Himself began their preaching with the word repent: *"Repent, for the kingdom of heaven has come near"* (Matthew 4:17). To repent means to change one's mind and turn in a new direction.

The first step toward repentance is feeling true sorrow for what we've done wrong. We read in 2 Corinthians 7:10, *"Godly sorrow brings repentance that leads to salvation and leaves no regret, but worldly sorrow brings death."* Worldly sorrow is like the regret of a criminal who's just been caught, whereas godly sorrow is the deep remorse or conviction that produces a change in direction.

Have you ever felt convicted after doing something wrong? The Bible says that the Holy Spirit is the one who convicts us of our sin (John 16:7–8). He gave us a conscience so we can know when we have sinned. Our conscience is our friend!

2. Believe that Jesus is God's Son and that God sent Jesus to pay the penalty for sin. There are three key verses to learn about this step in the salvation process:

> For God so loved the world that he gave his one and only Son, that whoever believes in him shall not perish but have eternal life. (John 3:16)

> Jesus answered, "I am the way and the truth and the life. No one comes to the Father except through me." (John 14:6)

> But God demonstrates his own love for us in this: While we were still sinners, Christ died for us. (Romans 5:8)

3. Confess your faith in Jesus Christ as Savior and Lord. Romans 10:9–10 tells us,

> If you declare with your mouth, "Jesus is Lord," and believe in your heart that God raised him from the dead, you will be saved. For it is with your heart that you believe and are justified, and it is with your mouth that you profess your faith and are saved. (Romans 10:9–10)

If this is the first time you've learned about the gospel, I would encourage you to accept it immediately. Tomorrow may never come for you, so there is no better time than the present!

God knows your heart. He knows if you are sincere and truly desire a change in your life. There are no magical words to say, no money to pay, no contracts to sign. It is a free gift from our Creator. All we need to do is accept it.

It'll be the best decision you'll ever make. Guaranteed!

If you'd like to accept Christ into your life right now, the following sample prayer will express your desire to make that change:

Dear Lord Jesus, I know that I am a sinner, and I ask for Your forgiveness. I believe You died for my sins and rose from the dead. I turn from my sins and invite You to come into my life. I want to trust and follow You as my Lord and Savior. Amen!

FIFTEEN
FINAL EXAM STUDY SHEET

> God proved His love on the cross. When Christ
> hung, and bled, and died, it was God saying to
> the world, "I love you."[19]
> —Billy Graham

When I was in school, I loved to use summary sheets to help me study for exams. These sheets provided brief summaries of the important points of a course so I could remember what was really important.

For the purpose of helping you remember the important points I've talked about, I've provided you with your very own cheat sheet. Imagine how quickly you could have gotten through this book if you had come straight to this chapter!

1. Accept the free gift of salvation. Ensure that you understand the gospel and that you have repented and accepted Jesus as your Savior.
2. Begin your journey immediately. Realize that death—or Jesus's return—could come at any time. Therefore, there is no better time than right now to begin your journey toward developing a

---

[19] Billy Graham, "God proved His love…" *Christianity.com*. Date of access: September 5, 2023 (https://www.christianity.com/wiki/christian-life/inspirational-christian-quotes.html).

close relationship with Jesus. Putting it off will result in spending eternity separated from Him in a place that is horrendous. Not making a decision to follow Him is in fact making a decision not to follow Him. It's catastrophic to die without building a relationship with Jesus.

3. Get to know Jesus. Read about Him in the Bible, particularly in the New Testament. Read other books about Him too. Watch videos and talk to others to really understand who Jesus is. Study Him like you're preparing for a final exam. Attend a Bible-believing church regularly.

4. Take time to listen. Carve out times during your day to simply listen to what God might want to say to you.

5. Talk to Jesus. Pray as often as you can throughout the day. Talk to Him about the good stuff and the bad. Talk to Him when you're driving, brushing your teeth, or walking your dog.

6. Exercise your faith. God loves when we fully trust in Him. Ask Him to guide you in everything you do.

7. Store your treasure in heaven. Focus on eternity, not just the present. The pursuit of money and possessions will not lead you to true happiness. Think about what will matter to you in a million years.

8. Rearrange your priorities, if necessary. Let your life and time management reflect what is really important. Is your relationship with Jesus the number one priority in your life?

9. Forgive. Deal with unforgiveness in your life. Forgive yourself and forgive others as Christ forgave you.

10. Pay attention to red flags. Are there things in your life that are hindering you from developing your relationship with Jesus? If so, deal with them as soon as possible. Let nothing stand in your way to growing closer with your Creator.

11. Protect yourself from the enemy's attacks. Be aware of your weaknesses and seek God's help in strengthening your life in these areas. Look to Him for strength and support.

CONCLUSION

Finally, brothers and sisters, whatever is true,
whatever is noble, whatever is right, whatever is
pure, whatever is lovely, whatever is admirable—
if anything is excellent or praiseworthy—
think about such things.
—Philippians 4:8

This book has told my story and explained how I came to the realization that my priorities were mixed up for most of my life. It's about how I learned *The Most Important Lesson* and changed my life so I can now focus on what's really important with the time I have left. It took me almost fifty-seven years to learn this lesson, unfortunately, but I consider myself the luckiest guy in the world to have finally learned it!

I hope I can save you precious time and effort by sharing my story.

God was gracious and merciful in giving me a second chance and bringing me back from the dead. He showed me mercy I didn't deserve. That's just who He is. He had every right to leave me dead on the floor of my living room, but He chose to give me a second chance to finally get things right with Him. He gave me a second chance so I could start studying the right material for the Final Exam.

I now realize that there is nothing more important than developing a close relationship with Jesus. Also important is the fact that He has asked me to share my experience and lessons with others.

My life has been an interesting journey ever since that fateful day when I died. Since then, life has not been one big happy fairy tale. We live in a fallen world where God's enemy works overtime to attack those who want to make a difference for His kingdom while they're still here on the earth.

In the two years it took me to write this book, I have encountered obstacles that sapped my motivation and caused me to struggle over what to write. I've also had mountaintop experiences with God when I have felt closer to Him than ever before. Other times I've felt like He was nowhere to be found, as though someone had built a huge wall between us.

During the difficult times, I've had to rely on what I know about God. The Christian faith isn't a religion based on feelings or rules; it's about building a relationship with the God who created us, loves us, and wants the best for us because He knows us best. Hebrews 13:5 confirms this: *"Never will I leave you; never will I forsake you."*

I know this to be true. I rested on this promise when times were tough. I know that my salvation and eternal destiny depend upon my choice to follow Him, no matter how bumpy the road gets. I have learned to trust the parachute and not in my own ability to save myself.

I also know that my timing is not always God's timing. He works things out according to His timing, despite how impatient I may be. His plans are *always* better than my plans!

My journey isn't over yet, and it won't be over until God calls me home for the final time—or better yet, until He returns in a cloud of glory like He has promised to do one day. It could be soon! Read Revelation, the last book of the Bible, to learn more.

My prayer is that I will be ready for that day. My prayer is that you will be ready for that day as well. Only you can know for certain whether you'll be ready.

Read God's Word, cover to cover. See what He has to say about getting your priorities straight and take His advice on how to build a close relationship with Jesus.

If the information in this book makes sense to you, share it with someone you love. As followers of Jesus, we are tasked with sharing His truth with as many people as possible. Would you throw a life preserver to a drowning loved one? Would you push them to safety if they were standing in front of an oncoming bus? Of course you would! It's a life and death decision. Their eternity is at stake.

I'd love to hear from you and hear how your journey is going. If you'd like, drop me an email at mostimportantlesson@gmail.com. In the meantime, I'll be praying for you!

Go with God,

Gary S. Edwards

APPENDIX:
HEART ATTACK SYMPTOMS

Symptoms of a heart attack include:

- Discomfort, pressure, heaviness, tightness, squeezing, or pain in your chest or arm or below your breastbone.
- Discomfort that goes into your back, jaw, throat, or arm.
- Fullness, indigestion, or a choking feeling (it may feel like heartburn).
- Sweating, upset stomach, vomiting, or dizziness.
- Severe weakness, anxiety, fatigue, or shortness of breath.
- Fast or uneven heartbeat.

Symptoms can vary from person to person or from one heart attack to another. Women are more likely to have symptoms like an upset stomach, shortness of breath, or back or jaw pain.

With some heart attacks, you won't notice any symptoms at all—this could be a silent myocardial infarction. This is more common in people who have diabetes.

Thousands of people die from heart attacks each year. In the United States, someone has a heart attack every forty seconds. Recognize the signs. Act quickly. You could save a life.

- Call 911 or your local emergency number immediately. Emergency personnel can start treatment enroute to the hospital.
- Stop all activity. Sit or lie down, in whatever position is most comfortable.
- Take nitroglycerin. If you take nitroglycerin, take your normal dosage.
- Chew and swallow aspirin if you are not allergic or intolerant (either one 325-milligram tablet or two 81-milligram tablets).
- Rest and wait. Stay calm while waiting for help to arrive.
- Keep a list of your medications in your wallet and by the phone. Emergency personnel will want this information.

RECOMMENDED READING

The following is a list of books you may find helpful in developing your relationship with Jesus.

Randy Alcorn, *The Treasure Principle* (Sisters, OR: Multnomah Press, 2017).

John Bunyan, *The Pilgrim's Progress* (London, UK: Stationers' Company of London, 1678, 1684).

Larry Crabb, Connecting: *Healing for Ourselves and Our Relationships* (Nashville, TN: Thomas Nelson, 2021).

John Eldredge, *Moving Mountains: Praying with Passion, Confidence, and Authority* (Nashville, TN: Thomas Nelson, 2017).

John Eldredge, *Walking with God: How to Hear His Voice* (Nashville, TN: Thomas Nelson, 2016).

Bob Goff, *Love Does: Discover a Secretly Incredible Life in an Ordinary World* (Nashville, TN: Thomas Nelson, 2012).

Skye Jethani, *With: Reimagining the Way You Relate to God* (Nashville, TN: Thomas Nelson, 2011).

R.T. Kendall, *Total Forgiveness* (Lake Mary, FL: Charisma house, 2007).

C.S. Lewis, *Mere Christianity* (London, UK: Geoffrey Bles, 1952).

Dr. Erwin Lutzer, *One Minute After You Die: A Preview of Your Final Destination* (Chicago, IL: Moody, 1997).

Gordon MacDonald, *Ordering Your Private World* (Nashville, TN: Thomas Nelson, 2017).

Reggie McNeal, *A Work of Heart: Understanding How God Shapes Spiritual Leaders* (Hoboken, NJ: John Wiley & Sons, 2011).

Deanna Oelke, *Deeper: Heart to Heart with Holy Spirit* (Calgary, AB: Deeper Ministries, 2018).

John Ortberg, *The Life You've Always Wanted: Spiritual Disciplines for Ordinary People* (Grand Rapids, MI: Zondervan, 2015).

John Ortberg, *Who Is This Man? The Unpredictable Impact of the Inescapable Jesus* (Grand Rapids, MI: Zondervan, 2012).

J.I. Packer, *Knowing God* (Westmount, IL: InterVarsity Press, 1993).

Eugene H. Peterson, *Leap Over a Wall: Earthy Spirituality for Everyday Christians* (San Francisco, CA: HarperOne, 1998).

Eugene H. Peterson, *A Long Obedience in the Same Direction: Discipleship in an Instant Society* (Westmount, IL: InterVarsity Press, 2019).

Dr. Rob Reimer, *Soul Care: Seven Transformational Principles for a Healthy Soul* (Franklin, TN: Carpenter's Son, 2016).

Stephen Smallman, *The Walk: Steps for New and Renewed Followers of Jesus* (Phillipsburg, NJ: P&R Publishing, 2009).

Tommy Tenney, *God Chasers* (Shippensburg, PA: Destiny's Image, 1999).

A.W. Tozer, *The Pursuit of God* (Christian Publications, 1982).

Carlos Whittaker, *Kill the Spider: Getting Rid of What's Really Holding You Back* (Grand Rapids, MI: Zondervan, 2017).

Dallas Willard, Hearing God: *Developing a Conversational Relationship with God* (Westmount, IL: InterVarsity Press, 2012).

Dallas Willard, *The Divine Conspiracy: Rediscovering Our Hidden Life in God* (New York, NY: Harper Collins, 2009).

Dallas Willard, *Renovation of the Heart: Putting on the Character of Christ* (Carol Stream, IL: NavPress, 2014).

ABOUT THE AUTHOR

Trained as a commercial pilot and teacher, Gary began serving in full-time Christian missions in 2002. He's a popular speaker at Bible camps and youth events and established his own cross-cultural, evangelistic ministry in 2011. Since then, he and his wife Joanne have been serving as directors of C-Quest Ministries in Progreso, Mexico, training and equipping church leaders in children's ministry and discipleship, hosting short-term mission teams, and assisting leaders in advancing their ministries.

Gary's conservative Christian upbringing provided the foundation for his future career path as an evangelist, missionary, and ministry leader. Admittedly, his DNA was all about doing things to further the Kingdom.

It took an unexpected cardiac arrest and life-changing death experience to finally teach Gary what he refers to as the most important lesson he's ever learned. He shares this lesson with his readers, hoping that it will transform their lives like it did his.